Excel
Get the Results You Want!

Year 5 Thinking Skills Tests

T0363253

**Sharon Dalgleish,
Tanya Dalgleish
& Hamish McLean**

PASCAL
PRESS

Completely new edition incorporating 2020 Selective School changes

Reprinted 2024

ISBN 978 1 74125 702 1

Pascal Press Pty Ltd
PO Box 250
Glebe NSW 2037
(02) 9198 1748
www.pascalpress.com.au

Publisher: Vivienne Joannou
Project editor: Mark Dixon
Edited by Mark Dixon and Rosemary Peers
Answers checked by Dale Little and Lyn Baker
Cover by DiZign Pty Ltd
Typeset by Grizzly Graphics (Leanne Richters)
Printed by Vivar Printing/Green Giant Press

Contents

ABOUT THIS BOOK

This book has been written to help develop students' thinking skills. Thinking skills involve two disciplines: critical thinking and problem solving.

Critical thinking means the ability to analyse a claim or argument; identify whether it is flawed or uses correct reasoning; and determine whether the evidence, assumptions and conclusion are warranted.

Problem solving as a thinking skill means the ability to use numerical or mathematical skills to work out solutions to problems. These include visualising and rotating solids in three-dimensional space; ordering a number of objects based on comparisons and characteristics; analysing graphs and diagrams; and solving mathematical puzzles involving numbers, shapes and time.

Critical-thinking and problem-solving skills are valuable in everyday life as well as in many fields of endeavour students might eventually embark upon.

The first section of this book teaches students 20 thinking skills. Each thinking skill is first defined, then a sample question is provided and the solution is worked through for the student as a teaching/learning exercise. Then two practice questions are provided. These are for the student to attempt independently. The solutions are worked through in the answer section of the book.

This section is followed by eight practice tests comprising 20 questions each. Each test includes an equal mixture of critical-thinking and problem-solving questions.

Answers and detailed explanations are provided at the back of the book. Most answers include the working out.

If you would like to use this book to help you prepare specifically for the Selective High School Test, you can merge two sample tests and have your child complete the two tests in 40 minutes.

One test will therefore comprise 40 questions, which is equivalent to the length of the Thinking Skills paper in the NSW Selective High School Placement Test. For example, you could merge Sample Test 1A with Sample Test 1B to form Test 1.

ABOUT THE SELECTIVE SCHOOL TEST

The NSW Selective High School Placement Test consists of four sections:

- **Reading** (30 questions in 40 minutes)
- **Thinking Skills** (40 questions in 40 minutes)
- **Mathematical Reasoning** (35 questions in 40 minutes)
- **Writing** (one question in 30 minutes).

The tests, except Writing, are in multiple-choice form, with each question being of equal value. Marks are awarded for each correct answer and applicants are advised to guess the answer if they are uncertain.

How the results are used by public schools

Entry to selective high schools is based on academic merit. In 2022 changes were made to the allocation of places. Under the Equity Placement Model, up to 20% of places are held for members of the following disadvantaged and under-represented groups:

- students from low socio-educational advantage backgrounds
- First Nations students
- rural and remote students
- students with disability.

It is important to remember that the places allocated under the Equity Placement Model will not necessarily be filled. In 2023, the first year of this new system, less than 10% of these places were offered. This means that more than 90% of the places were offered to general applicants. The new system has helped close the educational gap in participation from disadvantaged groups without having a significant impact on other applicants.

Students no longer receive a test score or placement rank. The new performance report will instead place students in one of the following categories:

- top 10% of candidates
- next 15% of candidates
- next 25% of candidates
- lowest 50% of candidates.

This change addresses privacy and wellbeing concerns including unhealthy competition between students. The sole purpose of the test is to identify students who would benefit from the chance to study at a selective school and, since it doesn't test knowledge of the curriculum, there is no diagnostic merit in the test—unlike the NAPLAN test, which can help identify areas where children can improve.

Minimum entry scores for selective schools are no longer published because these change from year to year and depend on the number of applicants, their relative performance and the number of families who decline an offer. Students placed on the reserve list no longer receive a numerical rank; instead an indication of how long it will take to receive an offer, based on previous years, is provided.

A selection committee for each selective high school decides which students are to be offered places. These committees also decide how many students are to be placed on the reserve list. Should a student with a confirmed offer turn down a place at a selective school, the place will be offered to the first student on the reserve list.

There is an appeals panel for illness or other mitigating circumstances. All applicants are advised of the outcome. The NSW Government provides detailed information on the application and selection process for parents on the Selective High School Placement Test. This is available from: https://education.nsw.gov.au.

ADVICE TO STUDENTS

Each question in the NSW Selective High School Placement Test is multiple choice. This means you have to choose the correct answer from the given options.

We have included a sample answer sheet in this book for you to practise on. Note that from 2025, however, the NSW Selective High School Placement Test will change to a computer-based test.

Some of the more challenging Thinking Skills problem-solving questions could take you up to 10 minutes to complete to begin with, as you may use diagrams or tables to help you solve them. Remember that the more questions you do of this same type, the faster you will become—until you know exactly how to solve them.

Thinking Skills sample answer sheet

Mark your answers here.

To answer each question, fill in the appropriate circle for your chosen answer.

Use a pencil. If you make a mistake or change your mind, erase and try again.

You can make extra copies of this answer sheet to mark your answers to all the Sample Tests in this book.

Test A

	A B C D		A B C D		A B C D		A B C D
1	○○○○	6	○○○○	11	○○○○	16	○○○○
2	○○○○	7	○○○○	12	○○○○	17	○○○○
3	○○○○	8	○○○○	13	○○○○	18	○○○○
4	○○○○	9	○○○○	14	○○○○	19	○○○○
5	○○○○	10	○○○○	15	○○○○	20	○○○○

Test B

	A B C D		A B C D		A B C D		A B C D
1	○○○○	6	○○○○	11	○○○○	16	○○○○
2	○○○○	7	○○○○	12	○○○○	17	○○○○
3	○○○○	8	○○○○	13	○○○○	18	○○○○
4	○○○○	9	○○○○	14	○○○○	19	○○○○
5	○○○○	10	○○○○	15	○○○○	20	○○○○

Identifying the main idea

- The main idea is the idea or conclusion the creator of the text wants you to accept is true. It's often stated at the beginning of a text but it could also be at the end or indeed anywhere else in the text. The rest of the text will support or add to— or give you reason to believe—this main idea.
- Read the question carefully and think about what the creator of the text wants you to accept. Underline the sentence you think could be the main idea. Check to see if the rest of the text gives you reason to believe this main idea. Read each answer option in turn to evaluate if it expresses the main idea. Quickly eliminate any answers that are definitely wrong. Decide which of the statements best expresses the main idea you found.

SAMPLE QUESTION

Birds of prey, or raptors as they are also known, are a group of birds that includes hawks, owls, eagles, vultures, falcons and more. They hunt and feed on animals like rabbits, rodents, fish, lizards and other birds. We already work to protect many kinds of animals but we need to do more to protect birds of prey. Birds of prey and their natural habitats face many human-caused threats. These include environmental pollution, urbanisation and the use of pesticides and rodenticides. Birds of prey are often shot or poisoned because they are seen as a threat or nuisance to communities. Some birds of prey are caught and kept in captivity as pets and for falconry, both legally and illegally.

Which statement best expresses the main idea of the text?

A Birds of prey are also known as raptors.

B We need to do more to protect birds of prey.

C Birds of prey can be found on every continent, except Antarctica.

D Birds of prey are often seen as a threat or nuisance to communities.

B is correct. The main idea the creator of the text wants you to accept is that we need to do more to protect birds of prey. The rest of the text supports this main idea by giving more information about the human-caused threats birds of prey face.

A is incorrect. This background information is used in the introduction but it is not the main idea.

C is incorrect. This information is not in the text so it cannot be the main idea.

D is incorrect. This is a reason to believe the main idea; it supports the main idea.

Practice questions

1 Nature-based therapy is beginning to make its way into modern treatments for some mental and physical health ailments, with some healthcare providers even 'prescribing' time in nature to their patients. This nature therapy can include things like tending to a garden, walking a dog, hiking through a forest, swimming in the ocean, or sitting or doing yoga in a park, and can be used alongside mainstream medical treatments. Medical research shows that nature therapy can reduce blood pressure and stress levels in patients, and that it has cardiac and pulmonary benefits. As little as five minutes in nature can improve your mood, self-esteem and motivation. Ongoing nature therapy can improve anxiety, addiction and more.

Which statement best expresses the main idea of the text?

A As little as five minutes in nature can improve your mood.

B Nature therapy is sometimes called forest therapy or eco therapy.

C Nature therapy can include things like tending to a garden, walking a dog or hiking through a forest.

D Nature therapy is beginning to be used as a modern treatment for some health ailments.

☞ **Answers and explanations on page 69**

Identifying the main idea

2 Dog's teeth and gums need care to prevent decay and illness. Dental and periodontal disease in dogs is extremely common. By the time they are just three years old, 80% of dogs will experience some level of dental/periodontal disease. Regular teeth cleaning is an important part of their healthcare and can improve their quality of life. The best way to prevent dental disease in your dog is to start brushing their teeth when they are a puppy—but never use human toothpaste. It has ingredients that can cause illness, and even death, in dogs. If in doubt, speak to a vet.

Which statement best expresses the main idea of the text?

A Dental and periodontal disease in dogs is extremely common.

B To brush a dog's teeth, use water or a small amount of flavoured dog toothpaste.

C Regular teeth cleaning is an important part of healthcare for dogs.

D It's best to start brushing a dog's teeth when they are a puppy.

☞ **Answers and explanations on page 69**

Identifying a conclusion that must be true

- To draw a conclusion you need to read and assess all the information and evidence provided. A conclusion can only be true if it is supported by evidence. A potential conclusion can be eliminated if there is evidence that contradicts it or if there is either no evidence or only incomplete evidence to support it.

- Read the question carefully. Judge which conclusion must be true based on the evidence in the text. As you read the answer options, try to quickly eliminate any potential conclusion that has evidence to contradict it. Also eliminate any conclusion that is neither proved nor disproved because the evidence is incomplete or unavailable.

SAMPLE QUESTION

In an online shopping survey, shoppers were asked if they've ever shopped online for washing machines, clothes dryers, microwave ovens or fridges. Survey results showed that anyone who shopped online for washing machines also shopped online for clothes dryers and everyone who shopped online for clothes dryers also shopped for microwave ovens but no-one who shopped online for a clothes dryer also shopped online for a fridge.

Davey, Lachie, Rebecca and Isobel completed the survey.

Based on the information, which of the following statements must be true?

A If Rebecca did not shop online for a washing machine, she did not shop online for a clothes dryer.

B If Isobel did not shop online for a washing machine, she did not shop online for a fridge.

C If Davey shopped online for a fridge, he also shopped online for a clothes dryer.

D If Lachie did not shop online for a fridge, he also did not shop online for a microwave.

B is correct. From the information given, anyone who shopped online for a washing machine also shopped online for a clothes dryer and (since they shopped online for a clothes dryer) they also shopped online for a microwave but not for

a fridge. It's therefore not possible for someone who shopped for a washing machine to have shopped for a fridge so B must be true.

The other answers are incorrect. These statements cannot be true.

Practice questions

1 Catriona, Julie and Leo all love smoothies and have their own favourite ingredients to use. Catriona loves using spinach, celery, apples, oranges and carrots. Julie loves using carrots, mangoes and oranges. Leo loves celery, mangoes, oranges, beetroot and carrots.

Which ingredients does Catriona love in smoothies that neither Julie nor Leo loves?
A beetroot and carrot
B celery and spinach
C apple and orange
D spinach and apple

2 Three dog breeders wanted to find out whose breed of dog was the fastest around an obstacle course. They each timed their fastest five dogs around the course. This is what they found:
- The fastest border collie was faster than the fastest kelpie.
- All the blue heelers were faster than most of the border collies.
- All the kelpies were faster than all the blue heelers.

Which one of these sentences can be concluded from the above information?
A The kelpies' average speed was faster than that of the other dogs.
B Border collies and kelpies will generally be faster than blue heelers.
C The range of speed was the greatest among the border collies.
D There was less of a range in speeds among the blue heelers than among the kelpies.

Identifying a conclusion that is not possible

- Before drawing a conclusion you need to consider all the evidence. For a conclusion to be true or correct it has to be supported by evidence. So you can work out when a conclusion is **not** possible or **cannot** be true because there won't be evidence to support it.
- Read the question text carefully. When working out your answer you should try to quickly eliminate any options that are obviously incorrect. In this type of question these will be the conclusions that are true. This will narrow down your choice.
- Judge which conclusion cannot be true by deciding which one has no evidence to support it.

SAMPLE QUESTION

If Archer does not go to band practice, then he likely won't be prepared for the big concert on Saturday.

If he isn't prepared, then he will not play well in the concert on Saturday. If he plays well in the concert on Saturday, then he might be offered a scholarship to continue his music lessons. Otherwise there is no way he will be offered a scholarship.

Which one of the following outcomes is **not** possible?

A Archer did not go to band practice but he was offered a scholarship.

B Archer went to band practice but he was not offered a scholarship.

C Archer was not prepared for the concert but he was offered a scholarship.

D Archer was prepared for the concert but was not offered a scholarship.

C is correct. From the information given you can draw the conclusion that if Archer is not prepared, there is no way he will be offered a scholarship. Therefore this conclusion cannot be true.

A is incorrect. This statement might be true. Although Archer didn't go to band practice, he might still be prepared for the concert and so could play well and possibly be offered a scholarship. The text says he will **likely** not be prepared, not that he **definitely** won't be prepared.

B is incorrect. This statement might be true. Archer might have gone to band practice but may still not have been offered a scholarship. They text says he **might** be offered a scholarship.

D is incorrect. This statement might be true. The information tells us that if all the conditions are met, Archer **might** be offered a scholarship, not that he will **definitely** be offered one.

 Practice questions

1 Five dogs were in the final run at an agility event. They had to run a course with 20 obstacles.
- Muffin was slower than Lola but Lola was slower than Joey.
- Joey was faster than Alfie but missed three obstacles.
- Fido cleared all the obstacles but took the longest.
- Alfie cleared more obstacles than Lola but finished after her.
- Lola finished second but missed two obstacles.

If all the above statements are true, only one of the sentences below **cannot** be true. Which one?

A Alfie cleared fewer obstacles than Fido.

B Joey was not the first to finish the course.

C Joey was faster than Muffin.

D Joey cleared the least number of obstacles.

2 **Blake:** 'Let's go to the mall after school.'
Amelia: 'I can't. I have to study for the test tomorrow. If I don't study, I'll probably fail.'
Blake: 'If you fail, Mr White will be in a bad mood!'
Amelia: 'Yes! But if he's in a good mood, I'm hoping he might let the class have a party. But if he's in a bad mood, there's no way he will let us.'
Which outcome is **not** possible?

A Amelia didn't study but Mr White said yes to the party.

B Amelia studied but Mr White did not let the class have a party.

C Mr White was in a good mood but he did not let the class have a party.

D Mr White was in a bad mood but he let the class have a party.

Identifying evidence that leads to a conclusion

- To draw a conclusion you need data or evidence that supports the conclusion. Sometimes you can't work out a conclusion because there isn't enough evidence.
- These types of questions ask you to identify which information allows you to know a conclusion. These questions are not asking you to draw a conclusion but instead to judge which option helps you to know the conclusion. You need to eliminate the options that won't lead to a conclusion or that don't help you work out a conclusion.

SAMPLE QUESTION

An environmental organisation decided to use single-use, plastic soft-drink bottles to create a giant beach sculpture to highlight the impact of single-use plastic on the environment. They asked all their members to vote for the animal to represent in the sculpture. Members were told to choose between an albatross, a turtle or a seal. Every member was given two votes. The winner would not necessarily be the most popular animal. The winner would be the animal that everyone voted for. If there was no animal that everyone voted for, then the environmental organisation would hold a second vote.

Every animal received at least one vote.

Knowing one of the following would allow us to know the result of the vote. Which one is it?

A Everyone voted for the seal or the albatross.

B No-one voted for both the seal and the turtle.

C The turtle was the most popular choice.

D Only two people voted for the seal.

B is correct. Since everyone had to vote for two of the three animals, knowing that no-one voted for both the seal and the turtle tells you that everyone must have voted for the albatross. B is the statement that allows you to work out the result of the vote which was that the sculpture will be of the albatross.

 Practice questions

1 Will's family wanted to choose a gift for their great-grandmother's 90th birthday. Everyone wanted to contribute and everyone wanted to be involved in choosing the gift so the family decided to have a vote. Everyone was allowed two votes and they had to vote for two different options. The family decided that the winning gift had to receive a vote from everyone. If no gift got everyone's vote, family members would have to choose individual gifts and there would not be a joint family gift.

The choices were:
- a personalised fleece blanket with every family member's name on it
- a jigsaw puzzle made of the front page of a newspaper from grandma's date of birth
- a book of photos of Grandma with each and every family member and their personal message to her.

Every gift received at least one vote.

Which of the following statements enables you to work out the gift Grandma received?

A Everyone voted for either the blanket or the puzzle or both.

B The photo album was the most popular vote.

C Only two people voted for the blanket.

D No-one voted for both the blanket and the photo album.

2 Tilly's friends decided to spend Saturday at the museum. They could walk, cycle or get the bus. They decided to have a vote as the fairest way to decide how to get there. Each person got two votes and they had to vote for two different modes of transport. They agreed to only accept one of the modes of transport if everyone voted for it. If this did not happen, they would have a revote. Every mode of transport got at least one vote.

Which statement below provides the evidence that allows you to work out the result of the vote?

A Everyone voted for either the bus or walking, or both.

B Cycling was the most popular choice.

C Only two people voted for the bus.

D No-one voted for both the bus and cycling.

Identifying an assumption

- An assumption is not stated in a text. It is something missing that has been assumed or taken for granted in order to draw a conclusion. An assumption is not necessarily true but the person making the assumption believes it is. For this reason, making assumptions can lead to incorrect conclusions.
- To identify an assumption in a text, read the text carefully and identify the conclusion that has been made. Next identify the evidence on which that conclusion is based. Finally read and think about each answer option. Which one of these options would you need to take for granted in order to draw this conclusion from the evidence?
- You can think about it like this:

EVIDENCE + ASSUMPTION = CONCLUSION

In order to answer the question you need to find the missing assumption to complete the equation.

SAMPLE QUESTION

> Hank arrives at his friend Violet's house. Violet is wearing overalls and is working on her car.

Hank: 'You love working on your car!'

Violet: 'No, I don't. It's such a nuisance! It broke down just as I was about to go out!'

Which assumption has Hank made in order to draw his conclusion?

A Violet is working on her car.

B Everyone who works on their car loves working on it.

C Violet's car broke down just as she was about to go out.

D Violet loves working on her car.

B is correct. For Hank's conclusion to hold, it must be assumed that everyone who works on their car loves working on it. (Violet is working on her car + everyone who works on their car loves working on it means therefore Violet loves working on her car.)

A is incorrect. This is the evidence Hank used to draw his conclusion.

C is incorrect. This is the real reason why Violet is working on her car, not the assumption Hank made.

D is incorrect. This is Hank's conclusion, not the missing assumption.

Practice questions

1 **Ramesh:** 'If we misbehave on the bus, it will hurt the reputation of our school.'

Talia: 'Here comes the bus now. We must behave when we get on!'

Which assumption has Talia made in order to draw her conclusion?

A Students from Ramesh and Talia's school often catch the bus.

B Ramesh and Talia must behave on the bus.

C Students must not do anything to hurt the reputation of the school.

D If Ramesh and Talia misbehave on the bus, it will hurt the school's reputation.

2 > When the local council suggested they would close the local public Sea Life Aquarium, Ms Small wrote a letter to the editor of the newspaper.
>
> Ms Small wrote: 'If the Sea Life Aquarium closes, it will hurt the local tourist economy. So we must keep it open.'

Which assumption has Ms Small made in order to draw her conclusion?

A We should not do something that will hurt the local tourist economy.

B The Sea Life Aquarium should not be closed.

C If the Sea Life Aquarium closes, it will hurt the local tourist economy.

D Ms Small likes visiting the Sea Life Aquarium.

Analysing reasoning to judge if it is correct

- When someone presents a point of view or makes a claim or an argument they use reasoning to support that point of view or argument. Their reasoning must make sense and be based on the facts available.
- When presented with a claim or argument, you need to decide what it is that the speaker or writer wants you to accept as true. Then you need to analyse their reasoning. If you accept that their reasoning is correct, you might accept their argument. If the reasoning does not make sense or is flawed, you can reject the claim or argument.
- These kinds of questions ask you to judge if the reasoning is correct. Read the question carefully. When working out your answer quickly eliminate answers that are obviously incorrect until you find the answer that is correct.

SAMPLE QUESTION

Students in 5M are given two marks in mathematical problem solving. One mark is for their ability in showing how to work out the answer to a problem and the second mark is for correctly answering the problem. Each area is marked out of 10 with an overall possible score of 20. This week Ricky and Angela got the same overall score for problem solving.

Ricky: 'If our marks in showing how to solve the problems were different from each other, then our marks in getting the answers correct must have been different too.'

Angela: 'And if our marks in getting the answers correct were the same, then our marks in showing how to solve the problems must have been the same too.'

If the information in the box is true, whose reasoning is correct?

A Ricky only

B Angela only

C Both Ricky and Angela

D Neither Ricky nor Angela

C is correct. Ricky correctly reasons that if the marks in one area were different but the scores in the other area were the same, then their results would not have been equal. Angela correctly reasons that if the marks in one area were the same but the marks in the other area were different, then their overall results could not have been equal. Both children use correct reasoning.

The other options are incorrect by a process of elimination.

 ### Practice questions

1 Two essential qualities needed to become a successful newsreader are an interest in current affairs and confidence in yourself.

Emma: 'Chloe would love to become a newsreader. She is passionate about public speaking and very confident but she is not very interested in current affairs so I don't think she'd be successful.'

Samesh: 'Charlie loves performing on stage and has great acting skills. He always checks the news and current affairs online. He'll make a great newsreader.'

Analysing reasoning to judge if it is correct

If the information in the box is true, whose reasoning is correct?

A Emma only

B Samesh only

C Both Emma and Samesh

D Neither Emma nor Samesh

2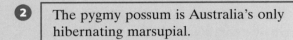

The pygmy possum is Australia's only hibernating marsupial.

Hannah: 'If you see a possum that seems to be asleep and you know it isn't a pygmy possum, then you know it can't be hibernating.'

Rowan: 'If you see an Australian marsupial and you know it is hibernating rather than asleep, then you know it must be a pygmy possum.'

If the information in the box is true, whose reasoning is correct?

A Hannah only

B Rowan only

C Both Hannah and Rowan

D Neither Hannah nor Rowan

☞ **Answers and explanations on page 70**

Identifying flawed reasoning

- When someone presents a point of view or makes a claim or an argument, they use reasoning to support that point of view or argument. Their reasoning must make sense and be based on the facts available.
- When you read or listen to a point of view or argument you need to analyse the reasoning. If the reasoning does not make sense or is flawed, you can reject the claim or argument.
- Some questions tell you the reasoning in a claim or argument is flawed. These kinds of questions ask you to identify the flaw or mistake that has been made. Read the question carefully. When working out your answer quickly eliminate answers that are obviously incorrect until you find the answer that is correct: the one that shows the flawed reasoning.

SAMPLE QUESTION

Sho volunteers at the animal shelter every weekend. The supervisor at the shelter has promised that any volunteers who did not have a chance to work in the puppy enclosure on the last roster will definitely be chosen to work in the puppy enclosure on the next roster.

Sho: 'The puppy enclosure is the best work area! But I worked there three times on the last roster. So that means I definitely won't be chosen to work there on the next roster.'

Which one of the following sentences shows the mistake Sho has made?

A Just because a volunteer did not get a chance to work in the puppy enclosure on the last roster, it does not mean that they would not have liked to work there.

B Just because a volunteer did not get a chance to work in the puppy enclosure on last roster, it does not mean that they will be given a chance to work there on the next roster.

C Just because Sho worked in the puppy enclosure three times on the last roster, it does not mean that he will be chosen to work there on this roster.

D Just because any volunteer who did not get a chance to work in the puppy enclosure on the last roster will be chosen to work there on the next roster, it does not mean that any volunteer who worked in the puppy enclosure on the last roster will not be able to work there again on the next roster.

D is correct. We know that any volunteers who did not have a chance to work in the puppy enclosure on the last roster will be chosen to work in the puppy enclosure on the next roster. However, this does not mean that anyone who worked there last roster will definitely not be chosen to work there again next roster. So this sentence shows the flaw in Sho's reasoning: he may still be able to work in the puppy enclosure on the next roster.

A is incorrect. This sentence is true and is not a mistake Sho has made.

B is incorrect. This sentence is a mistake, since the supervisor said they definitely will be given a chance to work there on the next roster. However, it is not a mistake Sho has made.

C is incorrect. This sentence is true and is not a mistake Sho has made.

Identifying flawed reasoning

 Practice questions

1 Krystal's mum entered a poetry contest at the local Writer's Festival. Each poet can enter only one poem in the contest. On the day of the Festival, each poet then gets three minutes to perform their poem in front of the live audience.

Mum: 'Judges score the poets and award ribbons for first, second and third place. Plus there is also a ribbon for People's Choice.'

Krystal: 'So that means four poets will get ribbons!'

Which one of the following sentences shows the mistake Krystal has made?

A One entrant might be awarded a ribbon for more than one poem.

B Some poets might be disqualified.

C The People's Choice ribbon winner might also come first, second or third.

D We don't know how many poets entered the contest.

2 There are two ways to qualify to enter the artistic gymnastics championship: by entering at least three local artistic gymnastics competitions during the year, or by winning an artistic gymnastics competition during the year.

This year, six students from Darren's school have qualified to enter the artistic gymnastics championship.

Darren: 'I know a total of four artistic gymnastics competitions were won by students at our school during the year. So that means more than half our qualifiers must be contest winners.'

Which one of the following sentences shows the mistake Darren has made?

A Some students who won artistic gymnastics competitions in the past may also have entered three other competitions during the year.

B Some of the students may have won more than one artistic gymnastics competition during the year.

C The number of artistic gymnastics competitions won during the year may be higher than in other years.

D Some students may have entered more than three artistic gymnastics competitions during the year.

Identifying additional evidence that strengthens a claim

- When someone makes a claim or presents an argument they use evidence to convince others to accept that claim. A claim can be strengthened with further evidence or additional information.

- To identify the statement that best supports or most strengthens a claim or an argument, read the text carefully. Identify the claim being made in the text. Then consider the answer options listed and assess the impact of each one on that claim. Look for the option that gives further evidence to support the claim or that most strengthens it. Try to quickly eliminate answers which are definitely incorrect or irrelevant to the argument.

SAMPLE QUESTION

Indigenous languages carry important cultural knowledge that is central to the identity of indigenous people around the world. It is vital to protect Indigenous languages from extinction. A language becomes extinct when there is no-one using it. It is predicted that half of the world's remaining 6500 languages will become extinct by the year 2100.

Some Aboriginal and Torres Strait Islander languages are in danger of extinction. One way to save a language is to record it and teach it in schools. Every Australian school should teach at least one Indigenous language to help save these languages from extinction.

Which one of these statements, if true, best supports the above claim?

A Teaching language in schools encourages and develops new users.

B It's too difficult to learn another language and not all children want to learn one.

C It's too expensive to implement language teaching in every school.

D It's irrelevant to preserve an endangered language if there's no-one left speaking it.

A is correct. The argument is that many indigenous languages are becoming extinct and could be saved by being taught in schools. This statement strengthens the argument because it
tells why it's important to teach an Indigenous language in Australian schools: to develop new speakers of these languages.

The other options are incorrect. These statements weaken the argument about teaching Indigenous languages in Australian schools.

Practice questions

1 Hibernation is a fascinating area of study with implications for human health. Animals which hibernate do so because weather conditions are especially difficult for survival or there is a lack of food. Some animals hibernate for months during the harshest winter temperatures or they hibernate briefly to stay cool in hot tropical temperatures. They might also hibernate for safety because hibernating helps them remain undetectable to a predator. Animals hibernate by slowing their heart rate down to five per cent to save energy. They are not sleeping. Scientists are working on ways to induce human hibernation to treat diseases such as cancer.

Which statement **strengthens** the above argument?

A Hibernation has the potential to be used in human medical practices.

B Bears can hibernate for up to 100 days.

C The first record of human hibernation was in 2006 when a Japanese man survived unconscious in the mountains for 24 days after an accident.

D Recent studies on blood flow during hibernation have led researchers to believe a major breakthrough in human hibernation research is likely.

2 A spokesperson says: 'In some parts of the world, due to wars, famine or natural disasters such as drought, it can be difficult for children to get enough food. This leads to malnutrition. The United Nations and other organisations provide communities with food packs of nutrient-rich foods such as peanut paste to help prevent malnutrition.

Which statement **strengthens** the spokesperson's claim?

A   Peanut paste is enriched with vitamins and protein powder.

B   Food packs can be transported and stored when necessary.

C   Malnutrition negatively affects children's physical and mental development.

D   Food packs help provide nourishment for children in need.

Identifying evidence that weakens an argument

- When someone makes a claim or presents an argument they use reasons or evidence to convince others to accept that claim.
- Any statement that calls into question or contradicts any of the evidence used to support a claim or argument will weaken that claim or argument.
- Firstly read the text carefully and identify the claim being made and the supporting evidence for that claim. Then assess which of the statements undermines or contradicts the supporting evidence or gives a reason why the claim is not valid.
- Look for the following:
  - □ a statement that contradicts evidence in the claim
  - □ a statement that undermines the accuracy of the claim
  - □ a statement that undermines or limits the scope of the claim
  - □ any statement that makes the claim less likely to hold up.
- When working out your answer, eliminate options that are incorrect until you find the answer that is correct

SAMPLE QUESTION

For the last 12 months the local Council has been trialling an off-leash dog area. A local dog owners' group now wants the council to extend the trial.

The group says: 'Having this designated area where dogs can play freely off leash ensures the safety of all our local dogs.'

Which one of these statements, if true, most **weakens** the group's claim?

A A report to Council found that the majority of local residents were in favour of the off-leash dog area.

B The off-leash area is located on a stretch of unfenced parkland next to the highway into town.

C The Council also trialled a two-way cycleway along the beachfront on the other side of town.

D The Council received very polarised feedback from the community about the off-leash dog area.

B is correct. The group claims the off-leash dog area ensures the safety of all local dogs. The fact that the area is unfenced and located next to a highway undermines this claim and therefore weakens it.

A is incorrect. This statement could strengthen a general argument in favour of extending the trial but it neither strengthens nor weakens the group's argument that the area ensures the safety of all local dogs.

C is incorrect. This statement neither strengthens nor weakens the group's argument about the safety of dogs in the off-leash area.

D is incorrect. This statement that there were divided views in the community about the off-leash dog area neither strengthens nor weakens the argument about the safety of dogs being ensured in the area.

Practice questions

1 The manager of a company announced to all staff that the company would not be replacing the biscuits in the company break room with fruit. The manager said: 'We have obtained quotes and fruit is a higher cost compared to biscuits. Fruit also does not store as well as biscuits. For these reasons the company has found that supplying fruit in the break room would be of little value to our staff.'

Which one of these statements, if true, most **weakens** the manager's argument?

A 90% of staff are in favour of fruit as a substitute for biscuits.

B Fruit does not last as long as biscuits.

C Staff were surveyed to find out what was the most popular biscuit.

D Fruit is more expensive than biscuits.

Identifying evidence that weakens an argument

2 **Charlotte:** 'Let's go to the Bayside Ocean Pool and swim some laps.'

Lucas: 'No way! It's the middle of winter! The water will be too cold to go swimming!'

Charlotte: 'Come on. It will be good for us. We've been studying all weekend and I need to do something to relax.'

Which one of these statements, if true, most **weakens** Lucas's claim?

A Swimming uses almost all the muscles in the body.
B Swimming has been shown to alleviate stress.
C Bayside Ocean Pool is not patrolled in the winter.
D Swimming in cold water improves your fitness and endurance because your heart must pump faster.

      ☞ **Answers and explanations on page 71**

Identifying an argument with the same structure

- When someone presents an argument they can structure it in various ways:
  - They can state their claim and provide evidence to convince others to accept that claim.
  - They can provide the evidence then conclude with their claim.
  - They can state their claim, provide evidence then restate their claim or make a call to action.
- To answer these types of questions you need to identify the argument that matches the structure of the argument given. You do not need to match the topic of the argument. Read the text carefully. Identify the structure of the argument then consider the answer options. Look for the option that matches. Try to quickly eliminate answers which are definitely incorrect.

SAMPLE QUESTION

Lucia: 'Apple pie is my favourite dessert because my grandmother used to make it for me when I was little and whenever I eat it, I think of her.'

Which argument below uses the same structure as Lucia's argument?

A **Sajid:** 'I prefer chocolate cake to apple pie because I love anything with chocolate in it.'

B **Viktor:** 'I rarely eat dessert because it is a sometime food and I try to control the amount of sugar I eat.'

C **Eliza:** 'Dessert should be a sometime food rather than an everyday food.'

D **Tash:** 'My grandpa makes soup out of all the vegetables he can find. He never wastes anything. He adds legumes to his soup too.'

B is correct. In her argument Lucia gives an opinion and then gives two reasons to support it. Viktor also gives an opinion and two reasons to support that opinion.

A is incorrect. Sajid only gives one reason to support his claim that he prefers chocolate cake.

C is incorrect. Eliza gives an opinion but no reasons to support this opinion.

D is incorrect. Tash describes her grandfather's soup objectively. She does not give an opinion about it so makes no claim or argument.

Practice questions

1

Climate change is causing more frequent and more severe bushfires each year and the bushfire season is beginning earlier in the year and lasting longer. Climate change must be addressed urgently.

Which of the following sentences has the same structure as the argument in the box?

A It's easy to recycle at least 95% of household waste if you separate materials and investigate local recycling options.

B The rate of mammal extinction in Australia is the worst of any continent on earth. Work needs to be urgently undertaken to prevent further extinctions.

C The country faces a nursing shortage because it hasn't been training or recruiting enough nurses.

D Fair Trade supports fair wages and working conditions for people in developing countries and works to ensure environmental and other protections. People should support Fair Trade.

2 **Maggie:** 'The RSPCA does a great job rescuing wildlife. Last week a member of the public contacted the RSPCA about a sugar glider on the train track. The Rescue Team took the glider to the Wildlife Hospital where it was discovered she had a sore eye. She's been treated and will stay with a carer until she is healthy enough to be released back into the wild near where she was found. If you notice an injured animal, contact the RSPCA.'

Identifying an argument with the same structure

Which of the following has the same structure as Maggie's argument?

A **Chris**: 'Baking a cake is a good way to support the RSPCA in fighting animal cruelty. I'm getting a fundraising team together again this year. Last year we raised nearly $500. The money helps the RSPCA rescue pets from situations where they are not getting proper care or are being mistreated.'

B **Jonah**: The RSPCA can suggest reward-based, force-free training methods for pets. There are classes held in most areas for humans and their pets.

C **Sophie**: 'The RSPCA does a great job in helping people and animals. The RSPCA's Homelessness program recognises that people who are homeless love their pets and need them as companions but might on occasion not have the ability to look after their pets. In these circumstances the RSPCA can find temporary foster care for the pets or help with veterinary treatment for the pets. The RSPCA really does understand how to care for people and animals.

D **Jamal:** The RSPCA says that training your puppy to walk without pulling on the lead is very important. You need to make the effort when your puppy is young.

Using Venn diagrams

- Many questions can be solved using what is called a Venn diagram. This type of diagram uses overlapping circles to help visualise and solve problems. While it is unlikely you will see a question with a Venn diagram in primary school, many problems asked of you can be solved by using one.
- There are a number of types of questions that can be solved using Venn diagrams. If you become familiar with them, you will be able to solve difficult questions far more easily.
- Venn diagrams are best used for questions where a person or thing can have more than one attribute. In the sample question, the members can like chess, checkers, both games or neither game. This means the group is split into four sections of a Venn diagram.
- The simplest Venn diagram and the one that you can use when solving questions in this book includes two overlapping circles inside a rectangle, as shown in all the solutions.

SAMPLE QUESTION

In a games club, 10 members were surveyed to find out whether they like chess and checkers.
- Seven members like chess.
- Five members like checkers.
- Two members don't like either game.

How many members like checkers but **not** chess?

A 0   **B** 1   **C** 2   **D** 3

B is correct.

This question seems confusing to begin with, as the total number of people mentioned is more than 10. However, some members have been counted twice. Some of them like chess as well as checkers, so have been included in both statements.

Let's look at a Venn diagram where the rectangle holds all 10 members and one circle holds those who like chess and the other holds those who like checkers. The overlapping section of the circles shows those who like both chess and checkers.

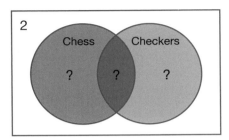

We can immediately put the 2 people who don't like either game in the rectangle but outside the circles. This means that there are 8 people left to put in the circles.

We are told that 7 people like chess and 5 people like checkers. There are 7 + 5 = 12 choices but only 8 spots. The extra choices must be for the people who like both. 12 − 8 = 4. This means 4 people have been counted twice as they like both chess and checkers. So we can put 4 in the overlapping section.

If 5 people like checkers and we already have 4 written in, then there is 1 more person who likes checkers but doesn't like chess. So the answer is B.

Similarly, there are 3 more people who like chess but not checkers.

The complete Venn diagram shows all 10 members, as all the numbers add to 10. There are 7 inside the chess circle, 5 inside the checkers circle and 2 not inside either circle.

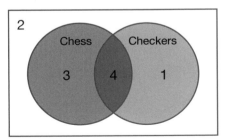

Using Venn diagrams

 Practice questions

1 A group of 12 guitar players were asked if they could also sing or play the piano. Five said they could sing, five said they could play the piano and five said they only played guitar.

How many of the guitar players can sing **and** play the piano?

A 2

B 3

C 5

D 7

2 A team of 22 Aussie Rules footballers were asked if they competed in swimming or in Little Athletics when they were children.

Ten players said they didn't compete in either of them. Ten players said they competed in swimming but five of those players said they competed in swimming only.

How many players competed in Little Athletics when they were children?

A 2

B 5

C 7

D 12

☞ Answers and explanations on pages 72–73

Questions with graphs

- Reading and understanding graphs is a difficult skill to master as graphs come in many different styles and can sometimes be misleading. These tests have questions about bar charts, column graphs and sector graphs (often called pie charts) but there are other graphs you may come across.
- Read each piece of information carefully. For the questions involving numbers, make sure to find out the scale used in the graph. This means you must check the scale on the side of a column graph and find out how many things are represented by each section in a bar chart. For questions on a sector graph, it is important to be able to identify whether a sector is a quarter circle, a sixth or an eighth of a circle.
- A key or a legend provides information for the reader of a graph. In some questions these may be left out on purpose to make the question difficult but you should be able to find what you need from the information given.

SAMPLE QUESTION

The British and Irish Lions Rugby Union squad is made up of players from four nations: England, Scotland, Wales and Ireland.

The graph below shows the distribution of players from each nation but the key showing which nation is which is not shown.

Nationality of squad members

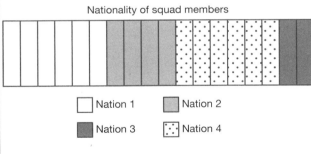

☐ Nation 1   ▨ Nation 2

■ Nation 3   ⸫ Nation 4

It is known that:
- a third of the squad is from Wales
- there are three times as many players from England as there are from Scotland.

If the squad is made up of 36 players, how many players come from Ireland?

A 4   **B** 8   **C** 12   **D** 16

B is correct.

There are 18 rectangles in the graph. If a third of the squad is from Wales, then Wales is represented by either the white or spotted sections as there are 6 rectangles in each and 6 is one-third of 18.

If there are three times as many players from England as from Scotland, then Scotland must be the 2 dark purple rectangles and England must be either the white or the spotted section, as 6 rectangles is three times as large as 2 rectangles. This means Ireland is represented by the 4 light-purple rectangles. Here is the graph with the key showing the nations:

Nationality of squad members

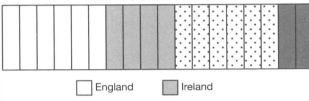

☐ England   ▨ Ireland

⸫ Wales   ■ Scotland

(In the key above, England and Wales could be swapped as they are the same size in the graph.)

There are 18 rectangles in the graph. If the 18 rectangles represent the squad of 36 players, then each rectangle represents 2 people: $2 \times 18 = 36$

There are, therefore, $2 \times 4 = 8$ players from Ireland.

☞ Answers and explanations on page 73

Questions with graphs

 Practice questions

1 A large group of students were asked to name their favourite creative subject at school. They could pick from art, music, drama, sewing, woodwork and metalwork.

A sector graph was created to show the results but the names of the subjects were left off and replaced with numbers.

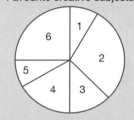

Favourite creative subjects

It is known that:
- more students liked art than anything else
- the same number of students chose sewing as chose metalwork
- twice as many students chose music than chose woodwork.

Which sector in the graph represents the people who chose drama?
A 3
B 4
C 5
D 6

2 Tony, Barry and Daisy had a competition to see who was the best goalkicker. They each had 10 kicks from four positions. The best goalkicker is the one who kicks most goals overall. Each friend is represented by a different colour in the graph below but it is not known who is represented by which.

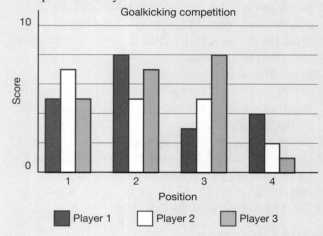

Barry kicked eight out of 10 goals from one of the positions. Half of Daisy's kicks were goals.

What is the smallest number of extra goals Tony needed to have kicked to be the outright best goalkicker of the three friends?
A 0 as he already had the most
B 1
C 2
D 3

☞ **Answers and explanations on page 73**

Determining the distribution of items

- These questions are very common in thinking skills tests. They involve a number of objects of one type being linked with a larger number of items of another type. For example, the sample question involves determining how many people had each of 0, 1 or 2 pairs of glasses.
- Sift carefully through the given information to find what is needed.
- For example, let's say that seven children choose to have one or two pieces of cake each. We also know that 10 pieces of cake are eaten.
- To find the number of children who have two pieces of cake, we subtract the seven children from the 10 pieces of cake. As $10 - 7 = 3$, there are three children who have two pieces of cake and so the other four children have just one piece of cake.
- You will use this exact method in almost all questions of this type, though you may have to do some other subtractions first. In the sample question you need first to subtract nine people who don't need any glasses before finding out how many people have two pairs.

SAMPLE QUESTION

An optometrist sees 38 people to decide if they need glasses. After the appointments the patients either need glasses or they don't. If they need glasses, they can purchase one or two pairs.

Nine people didn't need glasses at all. The optometrist sold 46 pairs of glasses.

How many people bought two pairs of glasses?

A 12   **B** 17   **C** 29   **D** 34

B is correct.

If 9 people didn't need glasses, then 29 people bought glasses: $38 - 9 = 29$.

To find out how many people bought two pairs we need to subtract the number of people from the number of pairs sold. This gives $46 - 29 = 17$.

As 29 people bought at least 1 pair, there are 17 pairs left over so 17 people must have bought 2 pairs.

Practice questions

1 After the theatre a school drama club of 40 students went to an ice-cream parlour. Students could order one or two scoops if they wanted.

Twelve students didn't get any ice cream.

The ice-cream parlour sold 36 scoops of ice cream to the group.

How many students got only one scoop?

A 8   **B** 16   **C** 20   **D** 28

2 A two-person chairlift operates at the Snowy Mountains. Each chair takes either 0, 1 or 2 people up the mountain. After 100 chairs had left the base of the mountain, 113 people had been taken to the top.

If 22 chairs were empty, how many people travelled up alone?

A 35   **B** 43   **C** 70   **D** 86

Solving 2D puzzles

- Many different types of questions can be asked about two-dimensional shapes. Often we are asked to find a missing shape that will complete a square or rectangle. In this book most questions will come with a grid to help you visualise how the shapes will fit together.
- Take note of how the given pieces will fit with each other and what features are on the sides of the pieces. Often pieces will have to be rotated so make sure to rotate them slowly in your mind, checking each feature of the shape is in the right place as you visualise it in a different position.
- Use simple sketches to get a good sense of what a shape should look like. For example, in the sample question you can lightly pencil in each shape on the grid to get the outline of the middle shape. You can do the same in questions without the grid like the second practice question here.

SAMPLE QUESTION

Five shapes go together to make a 4-by-4 square. Four of them are shown below, placed around the outside of a grid to help you.

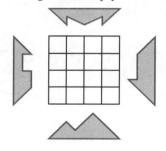

Which shape completes the square? Shapes may be rotated but not reflected.

B is correct.

By pushing the shapes shown into position on the square, the outline of the shape needed is revealed.

Practice questions

1 Five shapes go together to make a 5-by-5 square. Four of them are shown below.

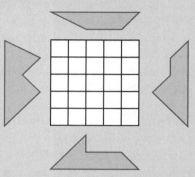

Which shape completes the square? Shapes may be rotated but not reflected.

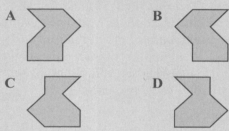

2 Four shapes go together to make a square. Three of them are shown below:

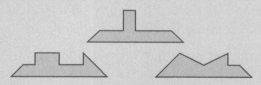

Which shape completes the square? Shapes may be rotated but not reflected.

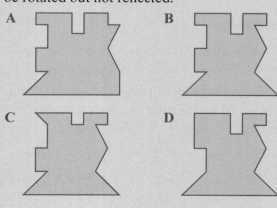

Identifying and following a pattern

- Identifying patterns made by the same shape but rotated or reflected is a common type of question. The questions in this book will focus mainly on patterns made with tiles of the same type.
- To identify patterns look across rows of tiles from left to right and ask yourself some questions. Are they rotating a quarter turn each move? Are they rotating a half turn? After how many tiles does the pattern repeat? You can do the same looking down the columns.
- There will also normally be a pattern down the diagonals. This can often be the best way to quickly spot which answer is correct. Sometimes it is easier to identify a pattern by looking at a square of either four or nine tiles.

SAMPLE QUESTION

The single-tile design above is used to cover the floor of a room in a repeating pattern. Four tiles are missing from the middle of the floor.

Which group of four tiles is missing from the blank spaces?

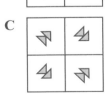

B is correct.

Notice the tiles are the same way up as we look up the diagonals from left to right. One diagonal is highlighted here for you:

This means the top-left tile of the four must be pointing to the top right. The bottom-right tile of the four must be pointing to the bottom left. The remaining two tiles must be pointing to the bottom right.

Practice questions

1

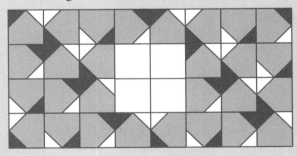

The single-tile design above is used to cover the floor of a room in a repeating pattern. Four tiles are missing from the middle of the floor.

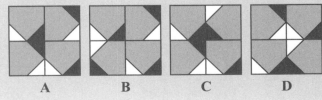

Which group of four tiles is missing from the blank spaces?

    A   B   C   D

Identifying and following a pattern

2 A number of blank tiles and tiles with arrows are arranged into a repeating pattern. There are nine tiles missing from the image shown.

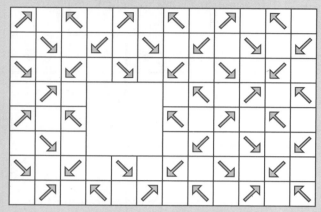

Which image below shows the missing nine tiles in the correct orientation?

A

B

C

D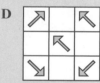

☞ **Answers and explanations on page 74**

Questions involving fractions of a quantity

- These questions require a good understanding of simple fractions like $\frac{1}{2}$, $\frac{1}{3}$ and $\frac{1}{4}$. Some questions require knowledge of more difficult fractions.

- The questions require you to find one fraction of a quantity when given another. For example, if we know that $\frac{1}{4}$ of the total number of people on a bus is 3 people, we can find out the total number of people by multiplying 3 by 4.

- The questions here are more difficult than this example but require the same thinking and skills.

- Some questions will mention a fraction of 'the remaining', meaning you need to take the fact that the quantity mentioned at the beginning of the question is now not the number which you are working with. The second practice question is one of these questions.

- It can be useful to work backwards through questions that talk about 'half of the remaining' and require you to work out the original number of people or things. A question may start with an unknown number that changes as a number of operations are performed. To find the unknown number you can perform the opposite operations from the final number to get back to the original number. For example, an unknown number has 3 added to it and the result is doubled to get 10. To find the unknown number, start at 10, halve it, then take 3 away. The unknown number is 2. This is because halving and doubling are opposite operations, and subtracting 3 is the opposite of adding 3. Notice that we did it in the reverse order too. The order matters.

- In the second practice question here, start working from the 6 passengers that remain on the bus.

SAMPLE QUESTION

A group of people were sitting at a railway station waiting for a train to arrive. When the train arrived four people got on the first carriage, one-quarter of the people got on the second carriage and the remaining half got on the last carriage.

How many people were waiting at the station before the train arrived?

A 6   B 8   C 12   D 16

D is correct.

The key to answering this question is to work out what fraction of the people is represented by the 4 people on the first carriage. To do this we need to know what fraction of the people got on the other carriages.

If $\frac{1}{4}$ and then $\frac{1}{2}$ of the people got on the second and last carriage, they represent $\frac{3}{4}$ of the people, as:

$$\frac{1}{4} + \frac{1}{2} = \frac{1}{4} + \frac{2}{4} = \frac{3}{4}$$

This means the 4 people who got on the first carriage represent $\frac{1}{4}$ of the people, as:

$$1 - \frac{3}{4} = \frac{1}{4}$$

So if 4 people is one-quarter, then $4 \times 4 = 16$ people were at the station.

🖉 Practice questions

1. Carla took a number of homemade necklaces to a market to sell. She sold them all in 3 hours. In the first hour she sold eight necklaces. In the second hour she sold half of the necklaces she took and she sold the last quarter in the third hour.

   How many necklaces did she take to the market?
   A 8
   B 16
   C 32
   D 48

2. There were some passengers on a bus. A quarter of the passengers got off at stop A. Three passengers got off at stop B. Half the remaining passengers got off at stop C, leaving 6 passengers on the bus. No-one got on at any of the stops.

   How many passengers were originally on the bus?
   A 12   B 20   C 24   D 30

Questions about time differences

- Time-difference questions can be very difficult. The questions in this book will mostly ask about the time differences between three cities. You may be asked to find the time in one city when given the time in another city or you may be asked to find the time difference between two cities.
- The best way to visualise and solve these questions is to draw a mini map, with the cities listed from left to right and those that are behind on the left and those that are ahead on the right.
- The difference between two cities can then be written on the map with a plus to show how many hours a city is ahead of another. You can see this in the sample question below.
- The sample question and the first practice question show the more difficult type of question, when it is a different day in the two cities given. Remember that if a city is ahead of another, it will hit midnight first and will therefore also start a new day first. Not all questions will require you to calculate over midnight.

SAMPLE QUESTION

Sydney is 10 hours ahead of London and London is 3 hours behind Moscow.

If it is 5:30 am on Tuesday in Sydney, what time is it in Moscow?

A 4:30 pm on Monday

B 10:30 pm on Monday

C 12:30 pm on Tuesday

D 10:30 pm on Tuesday

B is correct.

Sydney is ahead of the other cities so is written on the right. London is behind the other two cities so is written on the left.

The mini map is drawn below with the information shown about the differences between London and Sydney, and London and Moscow.

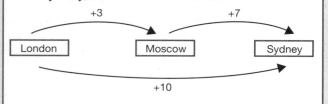

If London is 3 hours behind Moscow, then Moscow is 3 hours ahead of London. If Sydney is 10 hours ahead of London, then the difference between Sydney and Moscow is 7 hours. Sydney is 7 hours ahead of Moscow.

If it is 5:30 am in Sydney, you must subtract 7 hours to get the time in Moscow. You can do this in your head, taking 5 hours 30 minutes away to get to midnight and then 1 hour 30 minutes away to get to 10:30 pm the day before.

Practice questions

1 Yakutsk is 15 hours ahead of Winnipeg and Winnipeg is 2 hours behind La Paz. If the time in Yakutsk is 11:45 am on Wednesday, what time is it in La Paz?

  A 12:45 am on Thursday

  B 4:45 am on Thursday

  C 6:45 pm on Tuesday

  D 10:45 pm on Tuesday

2 When it is 5:30 pm on Tuesday in Phoenix, it is 7:30 pm on Tuesday in Lima. When it is 2:00 am on Sunday in Cairo, it is 7:00 pm on Saturday in Lima. What is the time difference between Phoenix and Cairo?

  A Phoenix is 9 hours behind Cairo.

  B Phoenix is 5 hours behind Cairo.

  C Phoenix is 5 hours ahead of Cairo.

  D Phoenix is 9 hours ahead of Cairo.

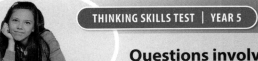

Questions involving rates of work

- The rate of work is a measurement of the amount of work done in a particular time. For example, a fruit picker might pick six bunches of bananas every 2 minutes. Combining rates of work is not easy and requires us to break down rates to their simplest parts. For example, it might be better to know that the fruit picker picks three bunches every minute, even though it is the same rate of work.

- To solve these problems, you will need to find the individual rates of work in terms of a common time. If I want to know how many bananas can be picked by a fruit picker and his friend, I need to find out how many each can pick per minute to solve the problem.

- Read the questions carefully and begin by setting the working out like the solution in the sample question.

SAMPLE QUESTION

Harry, Aaron and Louis are workers in a toy factory. Harry can make 12 toys per hour. Aaron can make 9 toys per hour and Louis can make 6 toys per hour. How long would it take the three of them to make 18 toys if they work together?

A 20 minutes

B 40 minutes

C 60 minutes

D 80 minutes

B is correct.

If we add together the number of toys each can make in one hour, we get 12 + 9 + 6 = 27. Together they can make 27 toys per hour. 27 and 18 are both multiples of 9 so, if we can find out how long it takes them to make 9 toys, we can use this to find out how long it takes to make 18 toys.

$$
\begin{array}{c}
27 \text{ toys in } 60 \text{ minutes} \\
\div 3 \qquad \div 3 \\
9 \text{ toys in } 20 \text{ minutes}
\end{array}
$$

This means they can make 9 toys every 20 minutes or 18 toys in 40 minutes.

 Practice questions

1 Together, Khaled and Mansoor can fold 100 paper cranes in 100 minutes. If Khaled folds at a rate of 45 cranes per hour, how many cranes can Mansoor fold in an hour?

A 5

B 15

C 25

D 55

2 Bryan and Cassandra want to make as many cupcakes as they can to sell at a stall. Their ovens are different sizes and can only fit a certain number of cupcakes. The recipe says to bake the cupcakes for 30 minutes. They each fill the ovens and bake for 2 hours, producing 200 cupcakes. If Bryan baked 128 of the cupcakes, how many cupcakes can Cassandra fit in her oven?

A 18

B 32

C 36

D 72

Finding the best price

- Many questions will ask you to find the best deal given a number of prices. Questions in this book will ask you which multiday passes should be purchased to cover a certain number of days. You will also be asked to find the best deal when buying many quantities of the same product, where larger quantities cost less.
- To solve questions involving dates, write out all days between the first and last day so you can see what you are doing. The sample question will require this method.
- In all questions it is good to find out which offer gives the best discount. For example, if a single can of drink is $3 and you can buy two cans for $5, it is cheaper **per can** to buy the two cans for $5, as they each cost $2.50. This is the basis of all the questions of this type.

SAMPLE QUESTION

A national park had the following prices for entry:

1-day pass	3-day pass	7-day pass
$8	$15	$25

Wilson needs passes for the following dates of the month: 3, 4, 7, 12, 13, 15, 18.

What is the cheapest combination of passes that will allow him to enter the park on all those days?

A $48   **B** $50   **C** $54   **D** $56

A is correct.

If two days were covered by 1-day passes, it would cost $16: 2 × $8 = $16. So a 3-day pass costs less than this. This means we should cover 2 days with a 3-day pass if we can.

A 7-day pass is $1 more expensive than three individual passes, so we wouldn't use it to cover three individual days. We would only use it to cover four individual days or more, depending on how spread out they are.

Looking at the dates listed below we can see the cheapest option.

1 2 <u>3</u> <u>4</u> 5 6 <u>7</u> 8 9 10 11 <u>12</u> <u>13</u> 14 <u>15</u> 16 17 <u>18</u>

      3-day   1-day   7-day

Wilson needs to buy one of each pass:
$8 + $15 + $25 = $48.

Practice questions

1 Caleb is sent to buy Anzac biscuits from a stall at a market. The prices are:

1 biscuit	3 biscuits	6 biscuits
$2.50	$6.00	$11.00

His mother gave him $20 and said he could keep the change after buying at least 8 biscuits. What is the maximum change that Caleb can keep?

A $0
B $2
C $3
D $4

2 A car park near Guido's work had the following prices:

1-day pass	2-day pass	5-day pass	7-day pass
$15	$25	$52	$70

Guido needed to park there every Monday, Tuesday, Wednesday, Friday and Saturday.

What is the lowest price for parking that Guido can pay every week?

A $65
B $67
C $70
D $75

☞ Answers and explanations on page 75

Determining different views of 2D shapes

- Being able to visualise shapes from different sides is an important skill and the following questions test your ability to visualise a different view of a 2D shape.

- If you are trying to visualise the opposite side of a 2D shape, everything will be reversed as if you are looking in a mirror. Move slowly along from left to right on a shape, checking right to left on the reflected image. Are there any shapes that aren't reflected that should be?

- Usually there will only be one or two things wrong with the options you are given. Once you have found them, you can use a process of elimination to find the correct answer.

SAMPLE QUESTION

Helen cut a large piece of cardboard into the shape of six trees. She stuck it in her window so it looked like there were trees outside her room. The view from inside her room is shown below.

What would the cardboard trees look like from outside the window?

A

B

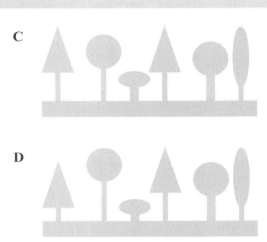

C

D

D is correct.

When looking at a 2D shape from the reverse side, it will appear as if the shape has been reflected. What is farthest to the left will now be farthest to the right.

A is incorrect. The trees are in the wrong order.

B is incorrect. The second tree from the right is too tall and has a thinner trunk than it should have.

C is incorrect. The tree on the far left is too tall and so is the tree third from the left.

☞ Answers and explanations on page 75

Determining different views of 2D shapes

Practice questions

1 Xian used plywood to create a forest backdrop for his school play. The view of the backdrop from the front is shown below.

What is the view of the backdrop from the reverse side?

A

B

C

D

2 Loulou cut out a piece of card for a model she was making. One side of the card is shown below.

What does the card look like from the other side?

A

B

C

D

20 MIN

1 Cameron and Ellie work at a cafe. Together they can make 15 coffees in 10 minutes. Cameron is a faster worker and makes eight of those coffees. If they work at the same pace for 1 hour, how many coffees will Ellie make?

A 7 **B** 35 **C** 42 **D** 70

2 Layne and Andreas are looking through the lost property box at school.

Layne: 'Maxi asked me to look for her jacket while we are here. It has a Torres Strait Islander flag on it but I can't seem to find it.'

Andreas: 'Look at that jacket—It must be hers. It has a Torres Strait Islander flag on it.'

Which one of the following sentences shows the mistake Andreas has made?

A There might be more than one jacket with a Torres Strait Islander flag on it.

B Maxi's jacket might not be black.

C Even though the jacket has a Torres Strait Islander flag on it, it might not be the right colour jacket.

D Maxi may have already searched the lost property box.

3 Finn and his friends are deciding what to order at a restaurant. Finn says: 'I'm trying not to eat meat anymore. Not eating meat is better for the planet.'

Which one of these statements, if true, best supports Finn's claim?

A Finn's favourite cricketer is vegetarian.

B There are a lot of choices that do not have any meat on the restaurant menu.

C A global study found that farming animals for food is the biggest cause of natural habitat loss worldwide.

D Research has shown that eating too much red meat can increase the risk of heart disease.

4 A city train network offers unlimited use for the following prices:

1-day	3-day	7-day
$25	$60	$120

Kara needs to use the train network on the following days of the month: 1, 2, 5, 6, 7, 9, 11, 12, 14 and 15.

What is the cheapest combination of passes she can use?

A $205 **B** $230 **C** $240 **D** $265

5 Toby's father is an author.

Lucy: 'Your father must have a good imagination!'

Which assumption has Lucy made to draw her conclusion?

A Toby wants to be an author.

B Toby's father has a good imagination.

C All authors have good imaginations.

D Toby's father is an author.

6 Four shapes go together to make a 4-by-4 square. Three of them are shown below.

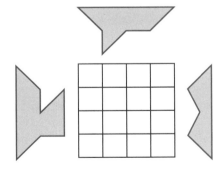

Which shape completes the square?

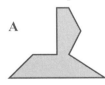 A

B

 C

D

7 Ivan, Killian and Bernie completed the weekly quiz in the newspaper over four weeks. The graph below shows their scores each week with each person represented by a single colour.

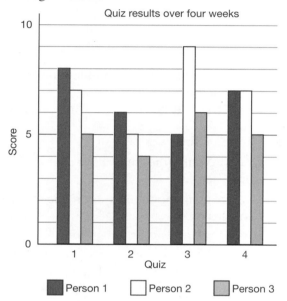

Quiz results over four weeks

■ Person 1 □ Person 2 ▨ Person 3

Killian got the same score in two of the quizzes. Bernie scored the same as Killian in one of the quizzes.

What was the difference between Ivan's best and worse scores?

A 2 **B** 3 **C** 4 **D** 5

8 Carlos, Jim and Lia live on the same street. They decide to hold a garage sale to sell their old toys. Carlos wants to sell a cricket bat, some books, a bike, Lego bricks and a magic kit. Jim wants to sell a science kit, a magic kit and Lego bricks. Lia wants to sell some books, a microscope, Lego bricks, a scooter and a magic kit.

What does Carlos want to sell that neither Jim nor Lia wants to sell?

A scooter and science kit

B cricket bat and bike

C bike and Lego bricks

D books and cricket bat

9 **Farid:** 'We should go to the swimming pool this morning. It's so hot! We could swim some laps and get some exercise. Then we could see a movie this afternoon if we feel like it.'

Which statement best expresses Farid's main idea?

A It's very hot.

B The weather forecast is for rain.

C They should go to the pool this morning.

D They could see a movie in the afternoon.

10 Students in a class of 25 were asked how many siblings they each had. Each student answered with either 0, 1 or 2. No students in the class were siblings of each other. The total number of siblings was 28.

If 10 students had two siblings, how many students in the class were an only child?

A 7 **B** 8 **C** 10 **D** 18

11

> A cumquat is an orange fruit. It can be round or oval shaped. It is smaller than a mandarin.

Mira: 'The fruit on that tree is orange and round. It might be a mandarin tree.'

Lee: 'But the fruit is very small. It could be a cumquat tree.'

If the information in the box is true, whose reasoning is correct?

A Mira only

B Lee only

C Both Mira and Lee

D Neither Mira nor Lee

12 Children are expected to show respect for and to obey their elders whether they are people in authority or just adults. Most adults believe this respect and obedience is essential but surely respect and obedience need to be earned and are not an automatic right. Just because someone is older does not mean they deserve respect or that they should be obeyed. The rules to obey your elders and only speak when you are spoken to are not relevant in modern times.

Based on the above information, which statement **weakens** the argument?

A Without respect and obedience children would behave badly and learn nothing.

B There needs to be a degree of automatic respect for older people because older people, especially parents, have earned respect and obedience.

C In modern times children are taught to question and to think critically for themselves.

D People need to earn respect.

13

The single tile design above is used in a repeating pattern to cover the floor of a room. Four tiles are missing from the middle of the floor.

Which group of four tiles is missing from the blank spaces?

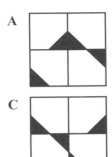

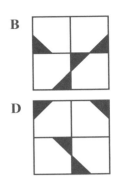

14 If Dane does not read the class novel, he won't be able to write a book review.

If he does not submit a book review, he will not be allowed to attend the author workshop.

If he submits a good book review, he's likely to be allowed to attend the author workshop and then apply for the author mentorship.

If he does not attend the author workshop, he will not be able to apply for the author mentorship.

If the above statements are correct, which one of the following is **not** possible?

A Dane did not read the class novel but still attended the author workshop.

B Dane attended the author workshop but did not get an author mentorship.

C Dane wrote a good book review but did not get a mentorship.

D Dane did not do well in his book review but was still able to attend the author workshop.

15 Chicago is 6 hours behind London. London is 3 hours ahead of Montevideo. If the time in Chicago is 4:20 pm on Sunday, what is the time in Montevideo?

A 1:20 pm on Sunday

B 7:20 pm on Sunday

C 1:20 am on Monday

D 7:20 am on Monday

SAMPLE TEST 1A

16 Isla, Eric and Cooper all collect stamps. Isla has stamps from China, Australia, Canada, New Zealand and Germany. Eric has stamps from South Korea, Germany and New Zealand. Cooper has stamps from Australia, Samoa, New Zealand, India and Germany.

What countries does Isla have stamps from that neither Eric nor Cooper has?

A India and South Korea

B Australia and China

C Canada and New Zealand

D China and Canada

17 Five shapes go together to make a circle. Four of them are shown below.

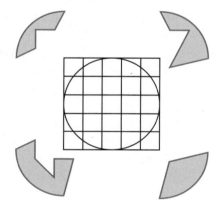

Which shape completes the circle? Shapes may be rotated but not reflected.

A   B

C   D

18 The local council has announced that a new pedestrian and cycle bridge will be built across the popular Black Lagoon. It will be built alongside the existing road bridge, which is a known danger spot for walkers

and cyclists. It is hoped the new bridge will solve these problems.

Which statement best expresses the main idea of the above text?

A A new pedestrian and cycle bridge will be built at Black Lagoon.

B Black Lagoon is popular in the local area.

C The new bridge will be higher than the existing bridge to reduce flood risks.

D The bridge at Black Lagoon has safety issues for walkers and cyclists.

19 An arrow is drawn in the corner of a square piece of paper as shown. The paper is then folded in half twice along the dotted lines before the arrow is cut out with an art knife.

When the paper is unfolded, what will it look like?

A    B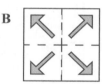

C 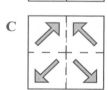   D

20 On Sunday Ben had some money in his wallet. On Monday he was given $5 pocket money. On Tuesday the amount of money he had in his wallet doubled after he did some chores. On Wednesday he bought some lunch for $7. He now has $23 in his wallet.

How much money did Ben have in his wallet on Sunday?

A $3

B $10

C $14

D $15

☞ Answers and explanations on pages 76–78

1 A shuttle bus company has the following rates:

1-day pass	2-day pass	5-day pass
$10	$16	$30

The passes run only for consecutive days.

Ahmad wants to use the bus on the following days of the month: 3, 6, 7, 9, 14, 15.

What is the cheapest combination of passes he can buy?

A $40

B $52

C $56

D $64

2

> To have any chance of winning a prize in the obstacle race you must have completed the course and cleared at least 10 of the 15 obstacles.

Noah: 'I completed the course and I cleared 10 obstacles. I'll win a prize for sure!'

Which one of the following sentences shows the mistake Noah has made?

A The obstacle race tests the strength, fitness and endurance of competitors.

B Doing the minimum required to win a prize does not guarantee a prize.

C Some competitors completed the course in personal-best times.

D Some competitors did not complete the course.

3 Grace, Violet and Valentino are competing in a fun run as a team. The competitors are to run around a course as many times as they can in 2 hours. Grace runs 20 laps of the course, Violet only runs six laps and Valentino runs around the course 14 times. Assume they run continuously at the same speed throughout the 2 hours.

As a team, how many laps had the team run after the first half hour?

A 5   **B** 10   **C** 15   **D** 20

4 Anya wants her school to get a therapy dog. Anya says: 'Having therapy dogs in schools is a good idea. Therapy dogs are friendly and relaxed. They can calm students who are upset. Therapy dogs make the whole school a happier place.'

Which one of these statements, if true, most **strengthens** Anya's claim?

A Therapy dogs help students feel more able to do things.

B Anya's teacher is allergic to dogs.

C Anya's friend goes to a school that has a therapy dog.

D Anya's mother is a dog trainer.

5 The shape below is placed on the grid.

Two other shapes are then placed on the grid and cover it exactly to make a square. Which two shapes below are they? Shapes may be rotated but not reflected.

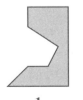

1   2   3   4   5

A 1 and 2   **B** 2 and 3

C 1 and 4   **D** 2 and 5

6 Ten students were asked if they owned a mobile phone or a computer.

Three owned neither. Four owned a mobile phone and five owned a computer.

How many students owned a computer but **not** a mobile phone?

A 2   **B** 3   **C** 4   **D** 5

7 A stall at a local weekend market displayed a sign:

> Our fruit tastes better!
>
> It's fruit that tastes like it did in your grandparents' day!
>
> Get in quick before we sell out!

Which assumption has the writer of the sign made to draw the conclusion on the sign?

A The stall owner wants to sell fruit.

B The fruit tastes like it did in the past.

C The fruit sold at the stall tastes better.

D Fruit tasted better in the past.

8 Ten dog owners at a park were asked how many dogs they owned. Answers ranged from one to three except for one owner who had five dogs. Together they owned exactly 20 dogs.

If two people owned three dogs each, how many people owned two dogs?

A 0   **B** 2   **C** 5   **D** 7

9 An environmentalist says: 'Christmas Island is one of the top ten natural wonders of the world. It is home to many unique and rare seabirds, land crabs and marine life. Once a year the island reminds us of its uniqueness when millions of red crabs come out of the forest. They swarm across roads and beaches as they make their way to the ocean.'

Which one of these statements best expresses the environmentalist's main idea?

A Christmas Island is an unspoilt tropical environment.

B Christmas Island is one of the top ten natural wonders of the world.

C Red crabs come out of the forest.

D We need to create a marine park around the island.

10 Garth read a book over three days. On the first day he read 15 pages. On the second day he read a third of the book. On the last day he read the remaining sixth of the book.

How many pages are in the book?

A 30   **B** 40   **C** 45   **D** 60

11 Boston is 5 hours ahead of Honolulu. Boston is 7 hours behind Kyiv. If it is 9:00 pm on Thursday in Honolulu, what time is it in Kyiv?

A 9:00 am on Thursday

B 7:00 pm on Thursday

C 11:00 pm on Thursday

D 9:00 am on Friday

12 **Mark**: 'Human referees and their assistants at sporting matches are not infallible. They cannot possibly see every moment in a game clearly and be able to make instant on-field decisions. Human referees also have their own biases for or against teams. Technology, including artificial intelligence, should be increasingly used to counteract human error and to ensure that matches, especially international sporting matches, are refereed fairly and accurately.'

Which of the following **weakens** Mark's claim?

A Artificial intelligence is not able to consider each player's feelings during a match and so would upset many of the players.

B The cost of implementing AI referees in all international sporting matches would be unaffordable.

C Referees sometimes need to adjudicate between players who have different opinions about an incident in a game and so only a human referee can judge which player is being truthful.

D A robot referee can keep its eye on the ball better than any human referee.

☞ **Answers and explanations on pages 78–81**

13 Lachie is deciding what to give his mother for Christmas. He says: 'I'd like to paint her a picture. But if I don't have time to paint, then I'll get her a book. And if I do paint, then I'll also get her a candle instead of giving her some vouchers.'

If Lachie does not give his mother a book for Christmas, what will he give her?

A a picture and a candle

B some vouchers only

C a candle and some vouchers

D a picture only

14 The skyline of some buildings along a street is shown below.

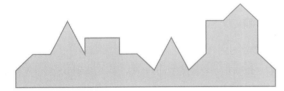

What would the skyline look like from the other side of the buildings?

A

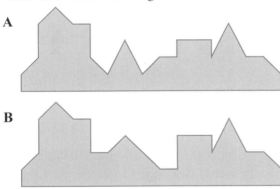

B

C

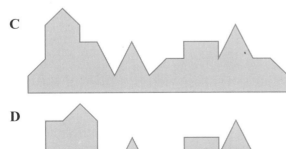

D

15 The Martuwarra Fitzroy River and catchment area is home to the critically endangered freshwater (largetooth) sawfish, 1500-year-old boab trees and endangered bilbies. Any extraction of water from the river for irrigation agriculture threatens the area's biodiversity. Martuwarra water must be protected from extraction.

Which of the following has the same structure as the argument above?

A The Martuwarra Fitzroy River is a significant First Nations heritage site and is Heritage listed for its outstanding cultural values. Any decision that has the potential to negatively impact the river undermines the unique rights of First Nations people. The Fitzroy River should be protected.

B The Martuwarra Fitzroy River and catchment area, occupying 93 000 square kilometres of Western Australia, is referred to by the traditional owners as the river of life. It supports 18 species of fish found nowhere else in the world, including the critically endangered freshwater sawfish.

C Urge your local Member of Parliament to protect the Martuwarra Fitzroy River and the livelihoods of local people, including the tourism industry. The Martuwarra Fitzroy River must be protected from extraction.

D Traditional owners of the land and water of the Martuwarra Fitzroy River catchment area oppose water extraction because it will drain the life-giving water from the natural environment.

16 Bangkok is 5 hours behind Suva and Suva is 1 hour ahead of Honiara. If the time in Honiara is 3:00 pm on Sunday, what time is it in Bangkok?

A 9:00 am on Sunday

B 11:00 am on Sunday

C 7:00 pm on Sunday

D 9:00 pm on Sunday

17 Wei found a leaflet in his letterbox. The leaflet advertised a new local store. The advertisement claimed:

'If you buy locally, it will help the local economy. So buy locally!'

Which **assumption** has the writer of the leaflet made to draw the conclusion in the advertisement?

A There is a new local store near Wei's house.

B People should buy locally.

C Helping the local economy is a good thing.

D Buying locally helps the local economy.

18

A large tennis club has 50 courts and rents them out at the same time. People can book the courts in groups of two or four, playing singles or doubles.

When the courts opened one morning, only five courts weren't being used. If 132 people were playing tennis, how many people were playing singles?

A 21	**B** 24
C 42	**D** 48

19 Jun and Harper each entered a photograph in a photography competition run by a local camera club. In the competition, entrants are allowed to enter only one photograph.

Jun: 'Judges score the photographs and award prizes for first, second and third. Plus there is also a special prize for best use of a feature from the local area.'

Harper: 'So that means four entrants will get prizes.'

Which one of the following sentences shows the mistake Harper has made?

A Some entrants might be disqualified.

B The special prize winner might also come first, second or third.

C We don't know how many photographs will use a feature from the local area.

D One entrant might be awarded a prize for more than one photograph.

20

Sara: 'Let's stay up late and binge that new horror series everyone is talking about!'

Thomas: 'I'd better not. I have to get an early night or I'll likely be tired for the audition tomorrow. I really want the lead in the new play. If I'm tired, I'll forget the lines.'

Sara: 'If you don't forget the lines, you might be offered the role. Otherwise you don't stand a chance! We can binge the show tomorrow night instead if you like.'

Based on the above information, which one of the following **cannot** be true?

A Thomas stayed up late with Sara but was offered the lead role.

B Thomas did not stay up late with Sara but was not offered the lead role.

C Thomas remembered all the lines but was not offered the lead role.

D Thomas was tired at the audition but was offered the lead role.

☞ Answers and explanations on pages 78–81

SAMPLE TEST 2A

20 MIN

1 Five shapes go together to make a 4-by-4 square. Four of them are shown below, placed around the outside of a grid to help you.

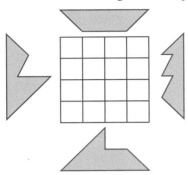

Which shape completes the square? Shapes may be rotated but not reflected.

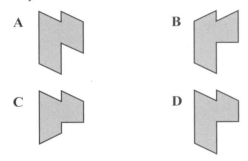

A   B

C   D

2 When Mei started horseriding lessons, her riding instructor told her: 'To have even a chance of being moved up into the advanced class you must have at least 40 hours of riding practice.'

If Mei's riding instructor is correct, which one of these statements will also be true?

A All the riders who have had 40 hours of riding practice will be moved up to the advanced class.

B Only the riders who have less than 40 hours of riding practice will be moved up to the advanced class.

C None of the riders who have less than 40 hours of riding practice will be moved up to the advanced class.

D Some of the riders who have less than 40 hours of riding practice will be moved up to the advanced class.

3 Ruby and Sam are telling their friends about their new teacher.

Ruby: 'He wears glasses.'
Sam: 'So he must be kind!'

Which assumption has Sam made to draw his conclusion?

A The new teacher must be kind.
B All people who wear glasses are kind.
C The new teacher wears glasses.
D Ruby and Sam have a new teacher.

4 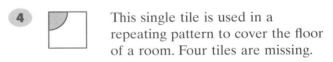 This single tile is used in a repeating pattern to cover the floor of a room. Four tiles are missing.

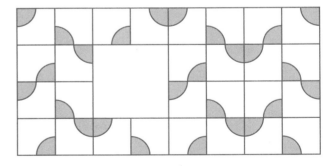

Which group of four tiles is missing from the blank spaces?

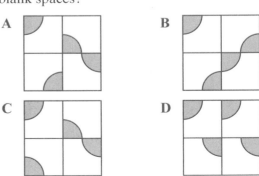

A   B

C   D

5 A vet says: 'Your cat's fur seems to be in poor condition with a strange smell. I've found the Hairy Cat brand of cat shampoo to be the best shampoo for a Devon Rex cat. I use it with my own cat and he has a thick, soft, nice-smelling covering of fur. I recommend 'Hairy Cat' for your pet. You can buy it through my clinic or order it online.'

Which of the following statements most **strengthens** the vet's claim?

A 'Hairy Cat' has been designed by cat experts for optimum cat hairiness and a good aroma.

B I've tried various other brands and they just don't give my cat the hairiness I'm after.

C Persian cats need the correct formula of shampoo for a healthy coat of hair.

D I get a commission on each bottle of 'Hairy Cat' I sell and I donate that money to the animal shelter.

6 Heidi, Charissa and Louisa are netballers. They took 10 shots from each of four positions to decide who was the best goal shooter overall. The graph below shows their results. Each person is represented by a different column colour.

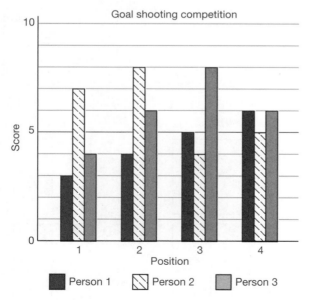

Heidi and Louisa scored the same from one of the positions. Charissa and Louisa scored the same overall.

Heidi scored one-third of her total at one of the positions. Which position was it?

A 1
B 2
C 3
D 4

7 A school photographer sells portrait photo packs to students.

Pack A comes with 1 large portrait.

Pack B comes with 2 large portraits.

Pack C comes with 3 large portraits.

The photographer sells 90 packs that comprise 165 large portrait photos. If he sells pack C to 10 students, how many students bought pack A?

A 25
B 30
C 55
D 110

8 **Zac**: 'Libraries should be closed. We don't need physical libraries with paper books anymore. People borrow audio books and digital books to read. Paper books cost trees and ink and are detrimental to the environment. Closing physical libraries will save land for other community uses. It will save state and council staffing costs as well as the paper and ink used in printing books. People can just order their books from a digital catalogue.'

Which statement most **weakens** Zac's argument?

A People like to read books for themselves.

B Libraries store printed books.

C Libraries are community centres and do more than just loan books.

D People need technology to borrow online.

☞ **Answers and explanations on pages 81–84**

9 Yusuf is entering his dog in a dog show that judges dogs on overall appearance, obedience and temperament. The prize for Best in Show is $100.

Yusuf: Monty is handsome, well behaved and cheerful. I'd award him the Best in Show prize money.

Arabella: Monty is all those things but that doesn't mean he'll be awarded Best in Show.

Paris: Yusuf loves his dog and is so proud of him. Yusuf always thinks Monty is the best-looking beagle he's ever seen.

Noah: Monty will win the show if he can show the judges that he is all the things Yusuf believes he is.

If the information in the box is true, whose reasoning is **incorrect**?

A Arabella

B Paris

C Yusuf

D Noah

10 In a street the buildings are either one, two or three storeys high. Half of them have only one storey. One-third of them have two storeys. The remaining seven buildings are three storeys high.

How many buildings are in the street?

A 21

B 35

C 42

D 70

11
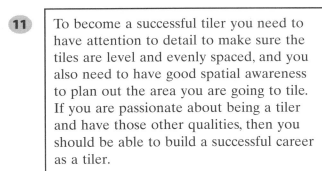
To become a successful tiler you need to have attention to detail to make sure the tiles are level and evenly spaced, and you also need to have good spatial awareness to plan out the area you are going to tile. If you are passionate about being a tiler and have those other qualities, then you should be able to build a successful career as a tiler.

Sage: 'Eddie loves working with his hands and helping his parents in their tile shop. He especially enjoys selecting and ordering tiles for sale in their store. He would likely not be a successful tiler because he does not have great spatial awareness.'

Greg: 'Mollie has great attention to detail when she knits. She creates patterns on jumpers where she has to draw the layout of the pattern on a grid. She also shows good spatial awareness when she draws her patterns. I think she'd be a successful tiler if she decided she wanted to be one.'

If the information in the box is true, whose reasoning is correct?

A Sage only

B Greg only

C Both Sage and Greg

D Neither Sage nor Greg

12 An expert on tropical diseases said: 'Mosquitoes are the deadliest creatures on earth. They kill more people through spreading disease than other animals do by biting, trampling or poisoning. Mosquitoes spread deadly diseases such as malaria, dengue fever, yellow fever and Zika virus. Malaria is the deadliest mosquito-borne disease. It kills more than 40 000 people each year.'

Which one of these statements best expresses the main idea the expert wants people to understand?

A Mosquitoes spread disease.

B Malaria is the deadliest mosquito-borne disease.

C People should protect themselves from mosquito bites.

D Mosquitoes are the deadliest creatures on earth.

13 If Auckland is 5 hours ahead of Perth and Dublin is 8 hours behind Perth, what is the time in Auckland when it is 4:15 pm in Dublin on Saturday?

A 3:15 am on Saturday

B 1:15 pm on Saturday

C 7:15 pm on Saturday

D 5:15 am on Sunday

14 If Jarrod doesn't measure the floor accurately, he might not order enough tiles.

If he runs out of tiles, he will not be able to complete the job this week and on time.

If he finishes the job on time, he might get a bonus payment.

But if the job is late, he won't get any bonus pay this week.

If the above statements are correct, which of the following statements is **not** possible?

A Jarrod did not measure the floor accurately but still completed the bathroom tiling job.

B Jarrod ordered enough tiles but did not complete the job on time.

C Jarrod completed the job on time but did not get a bonus payment.

D Jarrod did not order enough tiles but still got a bonus payment.

15 Three siblings decide to pool the pocket money they earn to buy a pet bird. The bird costs $90.

The eldest sibling earns $17 per hour. The middle child earns $11 per hour and the youngest child earns $8 per hour. One Saturday their parents ask them to clean the whole house.

If they start the day with no money, after how many hours of work together can they afford to buy the bird? They start the day with $0.

A $1\frac{1}{2}$ hours   **B** $2\frac{1}{2}$ hours

C 3 hours   **D** 5 hours

16 Ms Flint is a huge fan of the local basketball team. She watches them play every weekend and whenever they win, she always wears their team colours to school on Monday.

Louise: 'Ms Flint definitely wore the local basketball team colours to school last Monday. So they must have won last weekend.'

Arshan: 'Well, today is Monday and she isn't wearing the team colours. So they can't have won a game on the weekend.'

If the information in the box is true, whose reasoning is correct?

A Louise only

B Arshan only

C Both Louise and Arshan

D Neither Louise nor Arshan

17 A wildlife park has five different types of animal. It has many mammals, birds, fish, amphibians and reptiles. The sector graph below was made to show how many of each type of animal there are at the park but the names have been replaced by numbers.

Types of animal

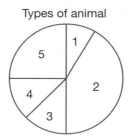

There are more birds than mammals and there are fewer amphibians than fish. There are twice as many mammals as there are reptiles.

Which animals are represented by sectors 3 and 4?

A fish and mammals

B mammals and reptiles

C amphibians and reptiles

D reptiles and fish

☞ **Answers and explanations on pages 81–84**

SAMPLE TEST 2A

18 Samir's mother wants to leave the city and build a more sustainable, off-grid house in the countryside. She wants the family to work together every weekend to build the tiny house. She says that, if they do this, they will be able to live without being connected to the electricity grid. They will be able to rely totally on solar energy.

Samir: 'But we can't live without our electronic devices! We need to charge them. I don't want to sacrifice anything!'

Which one of these statements, if true, most **strengthens** Samir's mother's argument?

A The system of solar panels will be expandable and can be added to if needed.

B During long periods of overcast weather it will be harder to charge the car.

C There will be a 165-litre solar hot-water unit.

D The house will be built with recycled and repurposed materials.

19 Mr Mosley wears some funny clothes to school. His students decided to note whether he wore clothes with spots and/or stripes over a 10-day period.

Mr Mosley wore spots on four days and stripes on seven days. On two days he didn't wear spots or stripes.

On how many days did he wear both spots **and** stripes?

A 1

B 2

C 3

D 4

20 Five shapes go together to make a 6-by-6 square. Four of them are shown below.

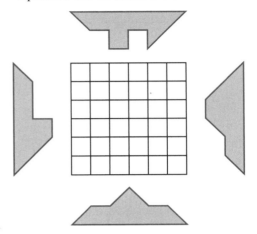

Which of the following shapes completes the square?

A  B

C  D

Answers and explanations on pages 81–84

20 MIN

1 Mr Young wants to buy some cherries from a stall on the side of the road. The prices are as follows:

500 g	1 kg	3 kg	6 kg
$8	$12	$30	$50

He only had $38 so he bought 3.5 kg of cherries. How much more could he have bought if he had double that amount of money? He may have change left over.

A 3.5 kg   **B** 4 kg

C 4.5 kg   **D** 5 kg

2 Dimitri said: 'Some sportspeople are paid very high salaries by sporting clubs. Sporting clubs obviously think the players are worth their salaries because these players can help their teams win. In my opinion, in a team sport every player dedicates skill, time and energy to being the best team member possible and team sporting matches are won or lost by the efforts of the whole team, so it's unfair to pay higher salaries to one or a few players.'

If the information above is true, which statement most **weakens** Dimitri's argument?

A Salary differences create jealousy in a team and are not good for team spirit.

B Players with more talent deserve to be paid for their talent.

C All sporting teams like to win and if a star player can help them win, they are happy for that player to be paid more.

D Some clubs cannot afford to attract star players with offers of high salaries.

3 Kiki, Dave and Simona are paving a backyard. Kiki can lay 57 pavers in an hour, Dave can lay 44 pavers in an hour but Simona can only lay 19 pavers in an hour. One hundred pavers need to be laid in the backyard.

How long will it take them to pave the backyard?

A 30 minutes   **B** 50 minutes

C 60 minutes   **D** 100 minutes

4 In an online survey of gym members' favourite classes it was found that everyone who liked yoga liked Pilates and everyone who liked Pilates liked spin, but no-one who liked Pilates liked crossfit.

Desi, Lia, Roman and Ivy completed the survey.

Based on the above information, which of the following statements must be true?

A If Roman does not like yoga, he does not like Pilates.

B If Ivy likes yoga, she does not like crossfit.

C If Desi likes spin, he also likes Pilates.

D If Lia does not like crossfit, she does not like spin.

5 Eleven cricketers were each asked if they liked batting or bowling best. Players were allowed to pick both if they liked them equally.

All of them picked something. Seven of them picked batting and six of them picked bowling.

How many picked both batting and bowling?

A 2   **B** 4   **C** 5   **D** 7

6 Skye, Brock and Abby completed a very difficult vocabulary test at the end of each term. The tests were out of 20. They recorded their scores on the graph below. Each student is represented by a different colour.

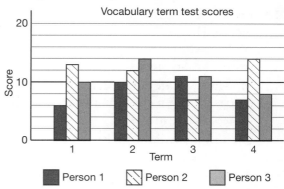

Skye's scores got worse each test until Term 4. Brock's scores got better each test until Term 4. What was the difference between Abby's best score and her worst score?

A 5   **B** 6   **C** 7   **D** 8

☞ **Answers and explanations on pages 84–87**

7 If Ben walks his dog, Fish, too far at midday then Fish is likely to be worn out.

If he is worn out, he will not be cooperative during his evening walk.

If he is cooperative on his evening walk, then he might get a treat. Otherwise he will not have a hope of getting a treat.

If the above statements are correct, which of the following is **not** possible?

A Fish was worn out and got a treat.

B Fish walked well in the evening but did not get a treat.

C Fish walked well at midday but did not go for an evening walk.

D Fish did not walk in the evening but still got a treat.

8 The owners of 143 houses on a street were asked how many cars they owned. Answers ranged from zero to two except for 10 owners who said they had three cars. Altogether the number of cars on the street was 180.

If 45 people owned two cars, how many people owned no cars at all?

A 28

B 60

C 88

D 90

9 Teff is a grain native to Ethiopia. Like other ancient grains, such as farro, quinoa, spelt, amaranth and millet, teff has been grown for thousands of years. It is an important crop for Ethiopia. 43% of Ethiopian farmers grow varieties of teff. In Ethiopia it is commonly used to make porridge and a thin, fermented, pancake-like bread called injera that is served with a spicey lentil stew. Teff cooks quickly so it is a more sustainable food than grains which take longer to cook because it cuts down on the amount of fuel required to prepare it.

Which of the following statements best expresses the main idea in the text?

A Ethiopians eat teff every day and sometimes three times a day.

B Teff is a good source of protein and so is an important food for Ethiopians.

C Teff can be grown with minimal water which makes it good to grow in a dry climate.

D Teff is an important crop for Ethiopia.

10 There are two ways to qualify for the national slam poetry competition. You could qualify by winning two regional events during the year or you could qualify if you have competed in an international event in the previous ten years.

This year six poets from Douglas's poetry group have qualified for the national competition.

Douglas: 'I know that three people who qualified have competed in international competitions during the past ten years so that means three of the poets who qualified must have won two regional events each during the year.'

Which one of the following sentences shows the mistake Douglas has made?

A Some poets may never have competed internationally.

B Some poets might have won an international event more than ten years ago.

C Some of the poets who qualified may have won more than two regional events as well as competed in an international event.

D Some poets who competed internationally may have won those events.

11

The single tile above is used to cover a floor in a repeating pattern, shown below.

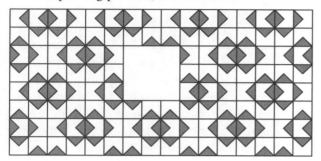

Which group of nine tiles is missing?

A

B

C

D

12 At a party there are 34 guests. Then 10 guests leave. After that a third of the remaining guests leave too.

How many guests remain?

A 13   **B** 16   **C** 24   **D** 26

13 A class decided to raise money for charity. They held a vote to decide which charity to choose. Class members could vote for UNICEF, the local animal hospital or the Cancer Council. Everyone in the class was allowed two votes but could not vote for the same charity twice. The teacher said they would only adopt a charity if everyone in the class voted for it because it was only fair that everyone would be happy with the outcome of the vote. If this did not happen, they would choose a different charity option instead.

Every charity received at least one vote.

Knowing **one** of the following would allow us to know the result of the vote. Which one is it?

A Every student voted for either the Cancer Council or UNICEF, or both.

B The animal hospital was the most popular vote.

C No student voted for both the Cancer Council and the animal hospital.

D Only two students voted for the Cancer Council.

14 A silhouette of a mountain range is shown below.

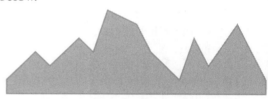

What would the mountain range look like from the other side?

A

B

C

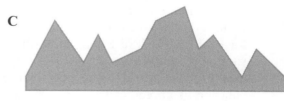

D

☞ Answers and explanations on pages 84–87

SAMPLE TEST 2B

15 Whoever washed the car must have had the time to do it and access to the car key.

If this is true, which one of these sentences must also be true?

A If Django had the time and the car key, he must have washed the car.

B If Django did not wash the car, it must be because he did not have the key.

C If Django did not wash the car, he cannot have had the time.

D If Django had the time and the car key, he might have washed the car.

16 Lalei cut a number of holes out of a piece of cardboard. This is the view of the cardboard from one side:

Which of the following is **not** a possible view of the back side of the card? The card could be rotated.

A    **B**

C    **D**

17
> Many of Australia's wildlife species rely on tree hollows for roosts and nest sites. It can take hundreds of years for these natural hollows to form. However, with land clearing, urbanisation and other impacts from people, there are fewer older trees and suitable hollows are harder to come by. We need to look after older trees and the important natural hollows that are left.

Which text below uses the same structure as the argument in the box?

A Kookaburras are believed to pair for life. Their nest is a bare chamber in a tree hollow. Every bird in a group of kookaburras shares the parenting duties.

B Once installed, nest boxes must be monitored. Unless a nest box is monitored it cannot be known how effective it is and which species, if any, are using it. Proper monitoring will also provide information about any damage to the box or any repairs needed.

C A nest box is an enclosure built especially for wildlife to nest or shelter in. It mimics natural hollows and provides a safe place for wildlife when no natural hollows are available. Our Aussie Nest Boxes are always evolving with improved designs to do just that. We are the best place to come to when you want to give wildlife a helping hand.

D To keep our precious wildlife safe, don't use rat poison or slug baits that accumulate in the food chain and inadvertently kill native wildlife.

18 Carlota did a study of 15 of the most popular chocolate bars around the world. Ten of them had caramel as an ingredient. Eight of them had nougat as an ingredient. Three of them had neither caramel nor nougat.

How many had caramel but no nougat?

A 2   **B** 3   **C** 4   **D** 6

19 Lola's teacher told the class: 'To have even a chance of winning a prize in our class readathon, you must have read for at least 20 minutes at least five times a week.'

If Lola's teacher is correct, which one of these statements will be true?

A All the students who have read for 20 minutes five times a week will win a prize.

B Only the students who have read for 20 minutes five times a week will win a prize.

C Some of the students who have read for less than 20 minutes each night will win a prize.

D None of the students who have read for less than 20 minutes five times a week will win a prize.

20 Ying and her friends have been watching an exciting series on television. The final episode is airing tonight. Ying wants to stay up late to watch it but her parents won't let her. They say it is too late to stay up on a school night.

Ying: 'There's nothing wrong with staying up late on a school night. All my friends do!'

Which assumption has Ying made to draw her conclusion?

A There's nothing wrong with staying up late on a school night.

B It's okay to do something if all your friends do it.

C All Ying's friends stay up late on school nights.

D Ying is not allowed to stay up late.

☞ Answers and explanations on pages 84–87

1 Four shapes go together to make a square. Three of them are shown below.

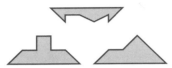

Which shape completes the square? Shapes may be rotated but not reflected.

A    B

C    D

2 Berries are very healthy. Nutritionists recommend eating half a cup a day to prevent diseases such as heart disease and Alzheimer's disease. The problem with this recommendation for many people is that berries can be quite expensive and many people cannot afford to eat berries every day, especially out of season. The government should subsidise berries so that people can eat them on a daily basis to improve their health and prevent disease.

Which one of these statements, if true, most **strengthens** the above argument?

A Investing in preventative health measures helps the economy because it's easier and cheaper to prevent disease than to treat it.

B Governments cannot afford to subsidise berries for people who want to eat them because that would cost the economy too much.

C Governments get their money from taxpayers who will never agree to subsidise the cost of berries.

D Berries are good for your health.

3 In a survey of aged-care residents about their preferences of flowers for the community gardens, everyone who liked succulents liked cacti and everyone who liked cacti liked banksia, but no-one who liked cacti liked roses.

Ethel, Aggie, Doris and Jorge all took part in the survey.

Based on the above information, which one of the following must be true?

A If Ethel likes banksia, she also likes cacti.

B If Jorge likes succulents, he does not like roses.

C If Doris does not like succulents, she does not like cacti.

D If Aggie likes roses, she does not like banksia.

4

The single tile above is used to cover the floor of a room in a repeating pattern. Four tiles are missing.

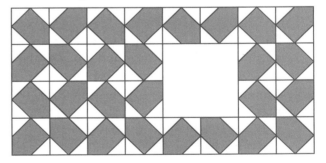

Which group of four tiles is missing from the blank spaces?

A 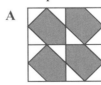   B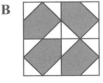

C 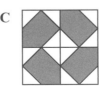   D

5 The greatest threat to the survival of coral reefs is climate change. Warmer water as a result of climate change leads to coral bleaching. Corals can recover from bleaching but it takes many years and continuous regular bleaching events leave coral with not enough time to recover. Climate change also leads to acidification of the oceans caused by the extra carbon dioxide in the water. Acidification devastates coral. Coral reefs are essential to the survival of over one million other species. Global action to address climate change is a matter of urgency.

Which statement best expresses the main idea in the text?

A Conservationists have discovered that coral can be grown in nurseries and then attached to damaged sections of the reef to restore it.

B Reefs are vital to support fisheries.

C Global action to address climate change is a matter of urgency.

D The greatest threat to the survival of coral reefs is climate change.

6 The person who ate all the chocolates and left the empty wrappers in the box must have had both an opportunity and a motive.

If this is true, which one of these sentences must also be true?

A If Kenny had both an opportunity and a motive, he must have eaten the chocolates and left the empty wrappers behind.

B If Kenzo did not eat the chocolates, he cannot have had an opportunity.

C If Kenzo did not have a motive, he cannot have been the one who ate all the chocolates and left the wrappers in the box.

D If Kenzo did not eat the chocolates, he cannot have had a motive.

7 A group of eight students were asked if they liked playing soccer and basketball.

Two students didn't like playing either sport. Five students liked playing soccer and five liked playing basketball.

How many students liked playing basketball but **not** soccer?

A 1   **B** 2   **C** 4   **D** 5

8 A tuk-tuk is a small taxi. There were 220 tuk-tuks on a street in Thailand. Some were empty and the remainder were carrying either one or two passengers. There was a total of 310 passengers.

If 108 were carrying one passenger, how many tuk-tuks were empty?

A 11   **B** 21   **C** 101   **D** 112

9 **Lana**: 'It's a waste of time, for the majority of students, to study maths past the basic level needed for Year 6 as most of us are never going to need complicated maths in our day-to-day lives or in our jobs.'

Which one of these statements, if true, most **weakens** Lana's argument?

A Educational institutions often require some level of maths for entry to any subject.

B Basic maths in useful in everyday life.

C There is less benefit in studying maths now than at any time in history.

D Some teachers don't help students appreciate the relevance of maths.

☞ Answers and explanations on pages 87–90

10 A number of guests went to a party. A quarter of the guests arrived early. An eighth of the guests arrived right on time. The remaining 15 guests arrived late.

How many guests attended the party?

A 15 **B** 24 **C** 30 **D** 36

11
> **Rose:** 'I'd rather play soccer than hockey because I find it difficult to hit the hockey ball with the hockey stick as my coordination is not that great.'

Which argument below uses the same structure as the argument in the box?

A Isla: 'I prefer watching track-and-field Olympic sports rather than equestrian events because I like to see people rather than animals compete.'

B Jana: 'I like the Paralympics better than the Olympics because the competitors have to work so much harder to achieve their goals.'

C Eric: 'I like dark chocolate better than milk chocolate because it's not as sweet and I've been told a little bit of dark chocolate is good for you.'

D Mohamad: 'I'd rather eat spinach than kale because it tastes better.'

12 Leilani's netball team decided to have an end-of-season party. They held a vote to decide on the venue. Team members could vote for three local venues: Pizza Palace, Sushi Central or Burger Basement. Everyone in the team was given two votes but they could not give two votes to the same venue. The coach said they should only accept one of the venues if everyone on the team voted for it because it was only fair that everyone should be happy with the outcome of the vote. If this did not happen, they would choose a different set of venues and have another vote.

Every venue received at least one vote.

Knowing **one** of the following would allow us to know the result of the vote. Which one is it?

A Everyone voted for either Burger Basement or Pizza Palace, or both.

B Sushi Central was the most popular vote.

C Only two students voted for Burger Basement.

D No student voted for both Burger Basement and Sushi Central.

13 Montreal is 5 hours behind Reykjavik and Santiago is 2 hours ahead of Montreal. If the time in Santiago is 10:00 am on Friday, what is the time in Reykjavik?

A 3:00 am on Friday

B 7:00 am on Friday

C 1:00 pm on Friday

D 5:00 pm on Friday

14
> Jess and Timmy received the same overall score in English for Term 2.
>
> The English score is made up of results in reading comprehension and a writing assessment. Reading and writing are both marked out of 50 so that the overall mark is out of 100 possible points.

Timmy: 'If we got different marks in reading, then we must have got different marks in writing too.'

Jess: 'If we got the same marks as each other in writing, we must also have got the same marks in reading.'

If the information in the box is true, whose reasoning is correct?

A Timmy only

B Jess only

C Neither Timmy nor Jess

D Both Timmy and Jess

15 Lloyd plays online chess and the game charges in the following ways:

Price	$10	$18	$80	$50
Games	50	100	500	Unlimited
Expires after	3 months	3 months	3 months	1 month

At first Lloyd signs up for unlimited games. After three months he changes what he buys when he realises he plays about 250 games every month.

How much can he save over the next three months by switching from the unlimited plan?

A $24

B $26

C $34

D $36

16

Noah's drama teacher said that any students who did not have a chance to perform in last term's play will definitely be offered a part in this term's play.

Noah: 'Oh no! I was the lead in last term's play. So that means I definitely won't be offered a part in this term's play.'

Which one of the following sentences shows the mistake Noah has made?

A Just because a student who did not have a chance to perform in last term's play will be offered a part in this term's play, it does not mean that any student who performed in last month's play will not be offered a part again in this term's play.

B Just because Noah had a part in last term's play, it does not mean that he will be offered a part in this term's play.

C Just because a student did not get a chance to perform in last term's play, it does not mean that they will be offered a part in this term's play.

D Just because a student did not get a chance to perform in last term's play, it does not mean that they would not have liked to perform in the play.

17 Carlos owns a coin collection. His coins come from four different continents: Asia, Europe, Africa and South America.

The following graph shows the number of coins from each continent in his collection but the key has been left off.

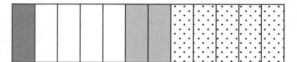

Carlos owns twice as many coins from Asia as from Africa. He owns 10 coins from Asia and 20 coins from South America.

How many coins from Europe are in his collection?

A 1

B 5

C 25

D 60

18 Mo says: 'We need to build a wildlife crossing over Forest Road to connect the bushland reserves on either side. It is hard for species to survive when roads leave their homes isolated. A crossing will help protect our valuable wildlife. The crossing could be made of ropes and cables above the road, linking to nearby trees so that tree-top species are not forced to the ground.'

Which one of these statements, if true, most **strengthens** Mo's claim?

A Ground-dwelling animals like echidnas need dry tunnels under roads.

B Light pollution from streetlights changes the natural environment and can have a drastic effect on animals.

C Mo wants to raise money to build the crossing.

D If tree-top species are forced to come to the ground to cross the road, they are in immediate danger from vehicles and predators.

19 Four friends named Nathaniel, Olivia, Peter, and Quinn each has a different height and shoe size.

- Nathaniel is taller than Peter but has a smaller shoe size than Quinn.
- Olivia is shorter than Nathaniel but has a larger shoe size than Peter.
- Peter has a smaller shoe size than both Nathaniel and Quinn.
- Quinn is taller than both Olivia and Peter, but shorter than Nathaniel.

One of the friends has the largest shoe size but is the shortest person. Who could it be?

A Nathaniel
B Olivia
C Peter
D Quinn

20 Four students are told to fold a square piece of paper in half along a line of symmetry. They are then told to do this exactly two more times. The paper is then unfolded.

If the dotted lines represent the creases made by the folds, which student didn't follow the instructions?

A 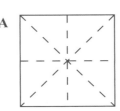 B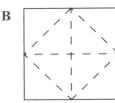

C 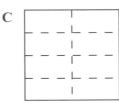 D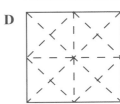

1 A ski resort had the following prices:

1-day pass	2-day pass	5-day pass	8-day pass
$120	$200	$400	$550

Lincoln wants to use the resort on Monday, Tuesday, Thursday and Saturday for two weeks in a row. What is the cheapest combination of passes he can use?

A $870

B $880

C $950

D $960

2 Both seals and sea lions spend time in the water and on land. They are pinnipeds, which means 'fin footed'. Sea lions are able to walk on land using their four large flippers. They can do this because their back flippers rotate forward and under their big bodies. Seals have back flippers that don't rotate. Therefore seals are fast in the water but on land they have to wriggle on their bellies!

Ria: 'That must be a sea lion on the beach. It's out of the water and it has four flippers.'

Max: 'No, it must be a seal. Look! It's on its belly.'

If the information in the box is true, whose reasoning is correct?

A Ria only

B Max only

C Both Ria and Max

D Neither Ria nor Max

3 The shape below is placed on the grid.

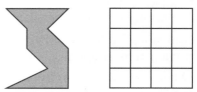

Two other shapes are then placed on the grid and cover it exactly to make a square. Which two shapes below are they? Shapes may be rotated but not reflected.

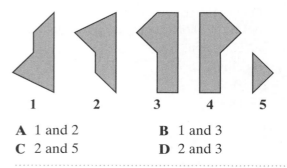

1   **2**   **3**   **4**   **5**

A 1 and 2   **B** 1 and 3

C 2 and 5   **D** 2 and 3

4 Marina's teacher says: 'Any student working in the garden should wear gardening gloves.'

Which one of these statements, if true, best supports Marina's teacher's claim?

A There is a box of new gardening gloves in the garden shed.

B You are less likely to get cuts or insect bites if you are wearing gardening gloves.

C All students will be working in the garden this term.

D Many different occupations require the use of protective gloves for workers.

5 Cameron did a study of 20 national flags. He noticed that 14 of them had blue on them and 10 of them had red on them. Four flags had neither blue nor red.

How many flags had red on them but **not** blue?

A 2

B 4

C 6

D 8

6 Ms Medcalf took a survey of where children at her school played during recess. Children can play on the oval, on the handball courts, on the basketball courts, on the play equipment, in the sandpit or in the library.

The results of the survey are shown in the sector graph but the play areas have been replaced by numbers.

Where students play

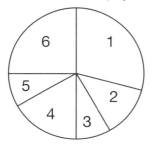

It is known that:

- More than a quarter of all students played on the oval.
- The same number of students played in the sandpit as played on the handball courts.
- Together those who played on the basketball courts and in the sandpit made up exactly one-quarter of the students.
- More students went to the library than used the play equipment.

Which play area is represented by sector 2?

A basketball courts

B sandpit

C play equipment

D library

7 The Southside sport field has received a long overdue upgrade. The playing surface has been renewed and changed to real turf. Environmental protection solutions have also been put in place to prevent the grass leaving the site. These include boot-cleaning facilities at exit gates and filters in stormwater pits.

Which statement best expresses the main idea of the text?

A The Southside sport field upgrade was overdue.

B Southside sport field has been upgraded.

C Southside sport field now has boot-cleaning facilities at exit gates.

D The hot rubber infill at the Southside sports field was replaced with cork.

8 A number of students were waiting to catch one of three buses home. Six students got on the first bus. Half the remaining students got on the second bus. The remaining 13 students got on the last bus.

How many students had been waiting before the first bus came?

A 19   **B** 26   **C** 32   **D** 38

9 A sporting club is entering a team in a charity car rally. The team wants to try to win the 'best-dressed car' prize. Club members were surveyed to find out what theme they would prefer to use to decorate the car. The survey found that everyone who liked safari also liked Smurfs. Also anyone who liked Smurfs liked hot dogs but no-one who liked Smurfs liked pandas.

Harvey, Lenny, Thao and Mari all took part in the survey.

Based on the above information, which one of the following must be true?

A If Harvey likes safari, he does not like Smurfs.

B If Lenny does not like pandas, he does not like hot dogs.

C If Thao likes safari, she does not like pandas.

D If Mari likes hot dogs, she also likes Smurfs.

10 Karl, Milla and Priya are three hairdressers who decide to open a shop and work together. Karl serves one customer every 20 minutes. Milla serves one customer every 15 minutes and Priya cuts the hair of two customers every hour.

What is the maximum number of customers they can serve in 8 hours?

A 37
B 56
C 72
D 90

11 Summer was walking to her favourite fishing spot at the river when she ran into her friend Carlos. Carlos was carrying a fishing rod.

Summer: 'I didn't know you fished.'

Carlos: 'I don't!'

Summer: 'Why are you carrying a rod then?'

Carlos: 'My dad asked me to fetch it for him.'

Which assumption has Summer made to draw her conclusion?

A Carlos is carrying a fishing rod to the river.
B Carlos fishes.
C Carlos is taking the fishing rod to his dad.
D Anyone who carries a fishing rod must fish.

12 The silhouette of a hillside is shown below. Treat all the trees as identical.

What would the hillside look like from the other side?

A

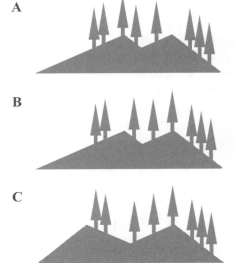

B

C

D

13 At a school performance night, parents could get a hot drink on arrival, at the intermission and at the end of the event. That is, they could choose to have up to three drinks each. Of the 80 parents who attended, only five parents didn't have a drink, while 11 parents had three drinks each. If 100 hot drinks were served in total, how many parents only had one drink?

A 3
B 25
C 32
D 61

☞ Answers and explanations on pages 90–94

SAMPLE TEST 3B

 14

In Goldtown there are two ways to qualify to sing in the choir for the Christmas show: by singing with the choir in at least three events or by winning a singing competition.

This year 15 students from Tom's school qualified to sing in the choir for the Goldtown Christmas show.

Tom: 'I know that eight singing competitions were won by students from our school during the year. So that means more than half our qualifiers for the Christmas show choir must be competition winners.'

Which one of the following sentences shows the mistake Tom has made?

A Just because someone qualified for the Goldtown Christmas show choir, it doesn't mean they want to sing in the show.

B The number of choir events during the year may be higher than in other years.

C Some of the qualifiers for the Christmas show may have won more than one singing competition.

D Some students may have sung in more than three events.

15 Ariane wanted to convince her boss to let her bring her dog to work with her. Ariane said: 'Studies show that having pets in the workplace can reduce stress and boost productivity.'

Which one of these statements, if true, most **weakens** Ariane's argument?

A One of Ariane's work colleagues is allergic to dogs.

B Doggie day care fees are very expensive.

C A pet-friendly workplace tends to improve staff morale.

D Ariane's boss does not own a pet.

16 Jess's father wanted to plant a native garden on the nature strip outside the apartment block where they lived. He spoke with the other residents in the building to see if they agreed with the idea.

Mr Small from the upstairs apartment said: 'That's a bad idea! No one will want to look after it. It will just get overgrown and look a mess or, worse, force pedestrians onto the road or block our view of the road when we try to drive out of the car park.'

Which one of these statements, if true, most **weakens** Mr Small's argument?

A Native gardens have more biodiversity than grass lawns.

B Nature-strip gardens should not block the vision of passing traffic.

C Once a native nature strip is established, maintenance is virtually nil.

D It is illegal to plant on the nature strip without Council permission.

17 Xavier had a number of cards that he used to play three games in a day. In each game you can win other people's cards by beating them and they can win yours.

After the first game Xavier had doubled the number of cards he owned. In the second game he lost eight cards to his opponent. In the third game he lost a third of the cards he owned, leaving him with 20 cards at the end of the day.

How many cards did Xavier start the day with?

A 11

B 19

C 30

D 34

18 Four students named Ahmed, Bethany, Chloe and Dustin sat a test. Each student completed the test in a different time and with different results.

- Ahmed finished the test before Bethany but got a lower mark.
- Bethany answered more questions correctly than Chloe but took longer to finish the test than Dustin.
- Chloe got a higher mark than Ahmed but took longer to finish the test than Bethany.
- Dustin answered fewer questions correctly than Ahmed but finished the test faster than Ahmed.

The person who scored the lowest, finished the test:

A fastest.

B second fastest.

C third fastest.

D slowest.

19 In the piano exam, students had to perform three pieces. The exam also included three extra components: sightreading, scales and an aural test.

- No-one passed all three extra components.
- No-one failed all three extra components.
- Everyone who passed scales also passed at least one of the other two extra components.
- No-one who passed sight reading failed the aural test.

Based on the above information, which one of the following **cannot** be true?

A Shayna passed scales and sight reading.

B Shayna failed scales and sight reading.

C Shayna passed only the aural test.

D Shayna passed scales and the aural test.

20 Ria and David both love to bake. This year they each entered a cake in the baking contest at the community fair. In the baking contest each entry is given a score for presentation and a score for taste. The two scores are then added together to give a final score.

Ria and David just found out that their cakes got the same final score.

Ria: 'If our cakes each got a different score for presentation, then our scores for taste must have been different too.'

David: 'And if our cake presentation scores were the same, then the scores for taste must have been the same too.'

Based on the information in the box, whose reasoning is correct?

A Ria only

B David only

C Both Ria and David

D Neither Ria nor David

☞ Answers and explanations on pages 90–94

SAMPLE TEST 4A

20 MIN

1 The local show is open for the first 10 days of the month. The prices for entry are shown:

1-day pass	3-day pass	5-day pass	10-day pass
$17	$35	$50	$88

Ivan wants to visit the show on the following dates: 3, 4, 6, 7, 8 and 10.

What is the cheapest possible combination of passes?

A $84

B $85

C $86

D $87

2 Tim sees his friend Mimi carrying a cake to school.

Tim: 'I didn't know it was your birthday today!'

Mimi: 'It's not my birthday! Dad made a cake for the fete tomorrow.'

Which assumption has Tim made to draw his conclusion?

A Students only bring cake to school on their birthday.

B It is Mimi's birthday today.

C There will be a cake stall at the school fete tomorrow.

D Mimi is carrying a cake to school.

3

Mr Lee: 'To have any chance of winning a prize in the quiz challenge, you must have completed all eight of this term's weekly homework quizzes.'

Sophie: 'I completed all eight quizzes. I'll win a prize for sure!'

Which one of these sentences shows the mistake Sophie has made?

A The quizzes were extra homework and not compulsory.

B Some students completed the quizzes in class.

C Doing the minimum required does not guarantee a prize.

D Some students did not complete all eight quizzes.

4 Five shapes go together to make a 5-by-5 square. Four of them are shown below.

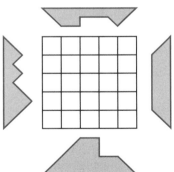

Which shape completes the square? Shapes may be rotated but not reflected.

 A

 B

 C

 D

5 Zoe's school was selecting students to attend a popular sustainability workshop. As well as considering students' previous school service, the school set students a community-service challenge and a Science test.

If a student had a record of previous school service, then they only had to pass the community-service challenge in order to be selected to attend. If a student did not have a record of previous school service, then they either needed an excellent result in the community-service challenge or they needed to do well in both the community-service challenge and the Science test.

Zoe had a good record of previous school service but failed to be selected to attend the sustainability workshop. What must have been the reason?

A Zoe did badly in the Science test.

B Zoe failed the community-service challenge.

C Zoe did not have a record of previous school service.

D Zoe did well in the community-service challenge but badly in the Science test.

6 A square wall has a number of differently shaped windows in it. From the outside it looks like this:

What would the wall look like from the inside?

A 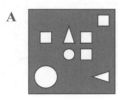 **B**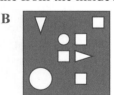

C 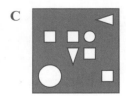 **D**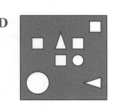

7 Ahmed surveyed the colour of the hair of the people at his work. He placed people into one of six categories. Hair was either dark brown, light brown, black, blond, red or other. Those in the other category had colourful dyed hair or didn't fit into the other five categories.

A sector graph was created to show the result but the colours have been replaced by numbers.

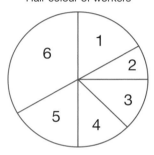

Hair colour of workers

It is known that:

■ Those with light-brown and dark-brown hair make up exactly half of the people.

■ The same number of people have blond hair as have dark-brown hair.

■ Those with red hair and other hair together make up less than a quarter of the people.

■ Those with blond hair and red hair make up exactly a quarter of the people.

Sectors 3 and 4 are the same size. Which two hair colours do they represent?

A black and other

B red and black

C blond and red

D dark brown and blond

8 A rowing club had eight boats. Some are singles (for one person only), some are doubles (for two people) and some are quads (for four people). When all eight boats are in use, there are 17 rowers out on the water.

If the club has more than one of each type of boat, how many doubles do they have?

A 2 **B** 3 **C** 4 **D** 5

9 Lina and Adam are discussing the impact of technology on society.

Lina: 'Technology has made our everyday lives better and there is nothing wrong with people's dependence on it.'

Adam: 'That's not entirely true. Technology has some negative impacts on society. Social media, for example, can cause harm if it is overused or misused.'

Which one of these statements, if true, most **strengthens** Adam's argument?

A Technology is all around us and not going anywhere so people need to get used to it.

B Research shows that the majority of negative impacts from technology come from its misuse.

C Research shows social media as the number one place for misinformation and hate speech, which leaves people feeling isolated and depressed.

D Social-media platforms are working to develop algorithms to detect deepfakes and to fight misinformation.

10 If it rains on Saturday, then the school fair will be cancelled.

If the fair goes ahead and is a success, we might be able to convince the principal to let us have another fair next term.

It won't be a success, though, if we don't have enough volunteers to work on all the stands.

If it isn't a success, then it will be the last fair we are allowed to hold.

If the above statements are correct, which one of the following is **not** possible?

A The Fair was not a success even though they had enough volunteers to work on all the stands.

B They did not have enough volunteers to work on all the stands but the principal let them have a fair next term.

C The fair was cancelled even though it did not rain on Saturday.

D The fair was cancelled even though they had enough volunteers to work on all the stands.

11 To be a successful volunteer assistance dog puppy educator, you need to enjoy learning, making friends and helping others succeed. You also need to be ready for a challenge and be able to handle dogs with confidence and patience.

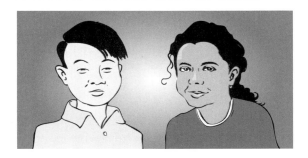

Matt: 'Beau was elected to the student representative committee at school and he always tries to help other students around the playground. He has a pet dog and in the school holidays he trained it to compete in agility. He'd be a successful puppy educator for sure.'

Kiah: 'Madi loves a challenge! She also has lots of friends from her volunteer work at the animal sanctuary and she helps out with the younger grades at school. But I don't think she likes dogs so puppy educator is definitely not for her.'

If the information in the box is true, whose reasoning is correct?

A Matt only

B Kiah only

C Both Matt and Kiah

D Neither Matt nor Kiah

12 Freetown is 5 hours behind Karachi and Tokyo is 9 hours ahead of Freetown. If the time is 11:00 pm on Wednesday in Tokyo, what time is it in Karachi?

A 9:00 am on Wednesday

B 7:00 pm on Wednesday

C 3:00 am on Thursday

D 1:00 pm on Thursday

SAMPLE TEST 4A

13 Ugly fish need our love and our help too. Marine life comes in all shapes and sizes and many species are under threat. But according to new research, we might not care about the ugly or odd-looking species enough to save them from extinction. The research found that the ugliest fish were the most at risk of dying out, even though they were more ecologically important. On the other hand, cute species attract more attention and more charity funding for conservation.

Which statement best expresses the main idea of the text?

A Ugly species, not just cute species, need our love and help to survive.

B Marine life comes in all shapes and sizes and many species are under threat.

C Cute species attract more academic research than ugly species.

D The ugliest fish are more at risk of dying out.

14 The owner of a large garden centre wants to redevelop the store to increase its capacity by adding a café, a children's playground, a pet store and extra parking. The owner argues that the redevelopment, with its increased capacity and provision of a range of complimentary uses, will improve the streetscape and enhance the surrounding locality.

Which one of these statements, if true, most **weakens** the garden centre owner's argument?

A The landscaping design of the redevelopment includes tree planting to contribute to the bushland setting along the road.

B The owner of the garden centre also owns other centres around the country and has been redeveloping these in line with the same business model.

C A pet store currently exists five minutes down the road from the garden centre.

D A new hospital next door to the garden centre is causing chaos in an area already under stress with too much traffic.

15 There are four friends named Emma, Fiona, Greg and Harry. No two friends have the same age or height.

• Emma is younger than Fiona but taller than Greg.

• Greg is taller than Harry but younger than Emma.

• Harry is older than Fiona but shorter than Emma.

• Fiona is older than Greg but shorter than Harry.

The youngest person is also the:

A tallest.

B second tallest.

C third tallest.

D shortest.

16

> Garry and Kai are on their school debating team. They are hoping their team will qualify for this year's State Debating Challenge. Any debating team that comes first or second in a regional competition during the year automatically qualifies. So does last year's State Debating Challenge winner, as long as the team still has the same members this year. There is also one 'wild card' team. This wild card team qualifies by being randomly drawn from all the debating teams that didn't qualify by the first two methods.

Garry: 'We won the regional competition but Lisa has now left the team. We have to convince her to come back. It's our only chance to qualify for the State Debating Challenge.'

Kai: 'No, that's not right. We could qualify by being drawn as the wild card.'

If the information in the box is true, whose reasoning is correct?

A Garry only

B Kai only

C Both Garry and Kai

D Neither Garry nor Kai

☞ Answers and explanations on pages 94–97

SAMPLE TEST 4A

17 Sonny and Shubham work at a burger bar. Together they can make 60 burgers in 90 minutes. Sonny is a faster worker and makes 36 of those burgers.

How many burgers can Shubham make on his own in one hour?

A 4   **B** 16   **C** 24   **D** 34

18 Pretoria is 10 hours ahead of Seattle and Port Moresby is 8 hours ahead of Pretoria. If it is midday on Monday in Seattle, what is the time in Port Moresby?

A 6:00 pm on Sunday

B 10:00 am on Monday

C 6:00 am on Tuesday

D 2:00 pm on Tuesday

19 Mr Ceric decided to investigate whether a 2-km walk before a test improved students' results in the test.

He split the class into two groups according to the alphabetical order of students' surnames. For the whole term students with surnames commencing with letters A to K were made to walk 2 km before every spelling test. Students whose names commenced with the letters L to Z did not have a walk.

When the teacher averaged out the results of the whole term's spelling tests, he found that, overall, students who had a walk before a test did better than students who did not have a walk.

Mr Ceric: 'It must be correct that walking before a test improves a student's results in a spelling test.'

Which one of the following shows Mr Ceric's mistake?

A The students who did not walk might have wanted to walk.

B There may have been more students with surnames commencing with A to K than those with surnames commencing L to Z.

C Some of the students might do a lot of exercise before school.

D The students who went for a walk might have been better spellers, on average, before the trial started.

20 Lyle and Kell are digging a trench. Lyle can fill 5 wheelbarrows full of dirt in 30 minutes while Kell can fill 2 wheelbarrows in 20 minutes. Working together, how long would it take them to fill 4 wheelbarrows with dirt?

A 4 minutes

B 10 minutes

C 15 minutes

D 25 minutes

1 A pizza parlour sells pizzas at the following prices:

1 pizza	$15
1 garlic bread	$7
Deal 1: 1 pizza + 1 garlic bread	$20
Deal 2: 2 pizzas + 1 garlic bread	$34
Deal 3: 3 pizzas	$40

Gabriel is given $90 to buy five pizzas and two garlic breads. What is the maximum amount of change that Gabriel can get?

A $7   **B** $8   **C** $9   **D** $10

2 Kale's mother wrote a letter to the local council arguing that the local ocean pool needs to be renovated. She said the pool needs a larger space for visitors to sit and enjoy the water views. She also said it needs a new 'living' seawall that would mimic the natural environment.

Which one of these statements, if true, most **strengthens** Kale's mother's argument?

A The pool was renovated last year.

B A living seawall at the pool would provide a home to seaweeds and shellfish.

C Kale's mother runs a cafe near the ocean pool.

D Research shows that ocean swimming improves mental and physical health.

3 A number of blank tiles and tiles with arrows are arranged into a repeating pattern. There are nine tiles missing from the image shown.

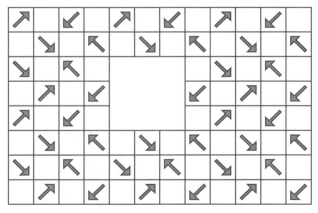

Which image below shows the missing nine tiles in the correct orientation?

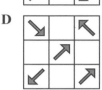

4 The Surf Cove local council wants residents to report any fox sightings. A fox and her cub were recently seen near Main Street. Sadly the Surf Cove little penguin colony is still recovering from a fox attack last year when 17 little penguins were killed. You can report fox sightings to the council's customer-service team.

Which statement best expresses the main idea of the text?

A A fox and her cub were seen near Main Street.

B Surf Cove residents should report fox sightings to the local council.

C Little penguins are an endangered species.

D Seventeen little penguins were killed by foxes last year.

5 A bag contained four types of lollies: lemon, chocolate, toffee and caramel. The following graph shows how many of each were in the bag but the heading and the key have been left out.

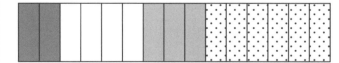

There were three times as many caramels as chocolates. There were three more lemon lollies than there were toffees.

There were exactly 12 of one type of lolly. Which was it?

A lemon   **B** chocolate
C toffee   **D** caramel

6 Fourteen people arrive at a restaurant that already contains some guests. After a small amount of time, a third of the guests leave the restaurant. There are now 12 guests left.

How many guests were in the restaurant to begin with?

A 4

B 6

C 12

D 18

7 The platypus is one of Australia's most unique animals so you would think it would be easy to identify one. But if it's at a distance, in bad light or you only get a quick glimpse, it can be difficult. One species often mistaken for a platypus in such situations is the rakali (Australian water rat). Rakali are mammals but they are adapted to aquatic habitats. They have dense waterproof fur and partially webbed hind feet. They are a similar size and colour to platypuses. They also sit quite low in the water when they swim. But the rakali's tail is long and thin compared to the flat, wide tail of the platypus.

Stella and Zac are participating in a citizen science project trying to spot a platypus in their local area.

Zac: 'If we spot what we think might be a platypus, it might not be. It could be a rakali.'

Stella: 'If we can't see the tail, we won't be able to say for sure if it is a platypus or a rakali!'

If the information in the box is true, whose reasoning is correct?

A Zac only

B Stella only

C Both Zac and Stella

D Neither Zac nor Stella

8 When it is 10:00 am on Friday in Mexico City, it is 11:00 pm on Friday in Hanoi. When it is 9:00 pm on Tuesday in Edinburgh, it is 4:00 am on Wednesday in Hanoi. What is the time difference between Mexico City and Edinburgh?

A Edinburgh is 20 hours behind Mexico City.

B Edinburgh is 6 hours behind Mexico City.

C Edinburgh is 6 hours ahead of Mexico City.

D Edinburgh is 20 hours ahead of Mexico City.

9 Mr Lees said: 'Whoever grew the tallest plant must have had a garden position with both good sunlight and good soil.'

If the above information is true, which one of these conclusions must also be true?

A If Emma did not have a position with good soil, she cannot have grown the tallest plant.

B If Nina had a position with both good sunlight and good soil, she must have grown the tallest plant.

C If James did not have a position with good sunlight, he must not have had a position with good soil.

D If Yusef did not grow the tallest plant, he must not have had a position with good soil.

10 Indira and Vashty are shearers. Together they can shear 50 sheep per hour. Indira shears a sheep every 2 minutes. How long does it take Vashty to shear a sheep?

A $1\frac{1}{2}$ minutes

B 2 minutes

C 3 minutes

D 5 minutes

11 Anita's father volunteers to work in the school canteen. The canteen supervisor emailed all volunteers and told them that any volunteers who did not have a chance to work in the canteen last month will definitely be put on the roster to work next month.

Anita's father: 'I worked in the canteen last month. So that means I definitely won't be put on the roster next month. That's good to know. Now I'll be able to organise the rest of my work.'

Which one of the following sentences shows the mistake Anita's father has made?

A Just because a volunteer did not get a chance to work in the canteen last month, it does not mean that they would not have liked to work in the canteen.

B Just because a volunteer did not get a chance to work in the canteen last month, it does not mean that they will be given a chance to work in the canteen next month.

C Just because Anita's father worked in the canteen last month, it does not mean that he will be rostered to work there next month.

D Just because any volunteer who did not work in the canteen last month will be put on the roster next month, it does not mean that any volunteer who worked in the canteen last month will not be put on the roster again next month.

12 Mr Barkley has a very interesting front door. It has a number of differently shaped glass panels in it. This is what it looks like from outside the house.

What will the door look like from inside the house?

A
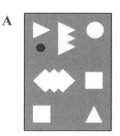

B
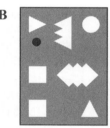

C
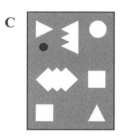

D
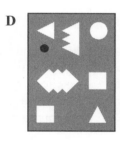

13 Gregory conducted a survey of the basketball singlets worn by the teams in his local competition. There are nine teams. Of them, five have red on their singlets and six have white. One team has neither red nor white.

How many teams have white but **not** red on their singlets?

A 0

B 1

C 2

D 3

SAMPLE TEST 4B

14 Five children did a word puzzle with up to seven rows to guess a word.

- Molly took longer to guess the word than Gemma but Gemma took longer than Lee.
- Lee was faster to guess the word than Gary but used all six rows.
- Baye used three rows but took the longest time to guess the word.
- Gary used fewer rows than Gemma but guessed the word after her.
- Gemma finished second but needed five rows to guess the word.

If the information in the box is true, which one of the sentences below **cannot** be true?

A Gary used more rows than Baye.

B Lee guessed the word before Molly.

C Lee was not the first to guess the word.

D Lee used the most rows.

15 Some people think guinea pigs are an easy option as a pet. But to be healthy, guinea pigs need exercise, environmental enrichment and mental stimulation. For physical and psychological wellbeing, their environment should let them express their natural behaviours, such as running, tunnelling, exploring, chewing, hiding, foraging and interacting with other guinea pigs. So get out there now and make a varied and interesting environment for your guinea pigs.

Which text below uses the same structure as the argument in the box?

A Buy Nature Pet Products. We only make pet food with real ingredients. No fillers, no hidden ingredients, no confusing labels.

B Guinea pigs should be given items to chew. This will keep them entertained. It will also wear down their constantly growing teeth.

C Guinea Pigs West End is the largest small animals store in the region. We stock all high-quality brands of food, plus cages, bedding and toys. There's really nowhere like us within a 100-km radius!

D Don't shop for a pet. Adopt a pet instead! Adopting a pet saves a life. Your new best friend is waiting. Visit Rescue Central today!

16 Kim, Lawrence, Monica and Neville competed in a hurdles race. They were the only competitors.

Kim knocked over fewer hurdles than Monica but finished faster than her.

Lawrence knocked over more hurdles than Neville and finished slower than him.

Monica finished faster than Lawrence and knocked over more hurdles than him.

Neville finished ahead of Kim but knocked over more hurdles than she did.

The person who knocked over the most hurdles finished where in the race?

A 1st

B 2nd

C 3rd

D 4th

17 The automatic sprinklers water the oval and gardens on Tuesday, Thursday, Friday and Sunday from 3 am to 4:30 am. A gardener is not needed on those days. On other days a Council gardener waters by hand from 7:30 am until 8:30 am. Watering is always completed early so that water soaks into the soil and does not evaporate too quickly when the day heats up.

At 8 am Ben looked for the gardener but she was not onsite.

Which of the following is the only option that must be correct?

A The gardener had finished watering.

B Today is Friday.

C The gardener is sick today.

D There was no watering today.

18 Francis, Grant, Heather and Ingrid are four farmers who each ran sheep and cattle on their farm.

- Heather has more sheep than Francis but fewer cattle than him.
- Grant has more cattle than Ingrid and fewer sheep than Heather.
- Francis has more cattle than Grant but fewer sheep.
- Ingrid has fewer sheep than Francis but more cattle than Heather.

The farmer with the fewest cattle has:

A the most sheep.

B the second most sheep.

C the third most sheep.

D the fewest sheep.

19

> Carly says she trekked up to Nunkeri Lookout on Sunday. She said it was a long trek but worth it for the beautiful view.
>
> There are three routes to the top. Two are of equal distance. One is the Coolibah Route and the other is via the Keating's Ridge rope bridge. The rope bridge partially collapsed during winter and has been closed by rangers for the past six weeks. The third route, the Waratah Route, is longer but safer.

Dani: 'Carly must have trekked the Coolibah Route because she said it was a long trek.'

Evie: 'She can't have trekked via the Coolibah Route because the rope bridge partially collapsed during winter and has been closed by rangers.'

If the information in the box is true whose reasoning is correct?

A Dani only

B Evie only

C Both Dani and Evie

D Neither Dani nor Evie

20 Robert has saved for an underwater camera to take on a family holiday to the Great Barrier Reef. He wants a lightweight camera that can stay underwater for long periods of time. He is budget-conscious.

Robert has narrowed down his choices to cameras that are all now available at Bill's Cameras, Smiths' Electrical, Horton St Hobby Shop or City Cameras.

The camera available at Horton St Hobby Shop stays underwater five minutes longer than the brands sold at Smiths' Electrical and City Cameras and 30 minutes longer than the brand sold at Bill's. The Smiths' Electrical camera is slightly heavier than the camera sold at Horton St but lighter than the one at Bill's Cameras. The one at City Cameras is the heaviest.

Which shop will Robert buy his camera from?

A Horton St Hobby Shop

B City Cameras

C Bill's Cameras

D Smiths' Electrical

IDENTIFYING THE MAIN IDEA

Page 1

1 **D is correct.** The opening sentence mentions this main idea and the rest of the text gives reasons to believe this idea.

A and C are incorrect. These statements contain supporting information for the main idea.

B is incorrect. This information is not in the text so it cannot be the main idea.

2 **C is correct.** The main idea is that regular teeth cleaning is an important part of healthcare for dogs. The rest of the text gives reasons to believe this idea.

A and D are incorrect. These statements contain supporting information for the main idea.

B is incorrect. This information is not in the text so it cannot be the main idea.

IDENTIFYING A CONCLUSION THAT MUST BE TRUE

Page 3

1 **D is correct.** Spinach and apple are both included in the list of ingredients Catriona enjoys in a smoothie that neither Julie nor Leo uses in their smoothies.

A is incorrect. Catriona does not use beetroot.

B is incorrect. Leo uses celery.

C is incorrect. Catriona uses apple and orange. However, both Julie and Leo also use oranges.

2 **C is correct.** You are told that all of the kelpies were faster than all of the blue heelers. Since the fastest border collie was faster than the fastest kelpie, the fastest dog must have been a border collie.

Since all the blue heelers were faster than most of the border collies, the slowest of the dogs must have been a border collie.

Since the fastest and slowest dogs were both border collies, it must be concluded that the range of speed must be greatest among the border collies.

The other answers are incorrect by a process of elimination.

IDENTIFYING A CONCLUSION THAT IS NOT POSSIBLE

Page 4

1 **B is correct.** It is helpful to record the known information in a chart like the one below:

Name	Fastest time	Obstacles cleared
Joey	1st	17
Lola	2nd	18
Alfie	3rd or 4th	19 or 20
Muffin	3rd or 4th	Not known
Fido	5th	20

This statement cannot be true. Lola finished second but was slower than Joey so Joey must have been first to finish the course.

A is incorrect. This statement could be true so it is not possible to say it **cannot** be true.

C is incorrect. This statement is true.

D is incorrect. We don't know whether this statement is true or not, since we do not know how many obstacles Muffin cleared. Therefore it is not possible to say it **cannot** be true.

2 **D is correct.** From the information given you can draw the conclusion that if Mr White was in a bad mood, there was no way he would let the class have a party. So this conclusion cannot be true.

A is incorrect. This statement might be true. Although Amelia did not study, she might still have passed the test and Mr White might not have been in a bad mood. And if Mr White was in a good mood, he might have let the class have a party.

B is incorrect. This statement might be true. Amelia might have studied but still failed the test. Or she might have studied and passed the test but Mr White could still have been in a bad mood.

C is incorrect. This statement might be true. The information tells us that if Mr White was in a good mood, he **might** let the class have a party—not that he will **definitely** let them.

IDENTIFYING EVIDENCE THAT LEADS TO A CONCLUSION

Page 5

1   **D is correct.** Since everyone had to vote for two of the three gifts, knowing that no-one voted for both the blanket and the photo album tells you that everyone must have voted for the jigsaw puzzle. The outcome will therefore be to buy the jigsaw puzzle.

2   **D is correct.** Since everyone had to vote for two of the three modes of transport, knowing that no-one voted for both the bus and cycling tells you that everyone must have voted for walking. D is the statement that allows you to work out the result of the vote: that the friends will walk to the museum.

IDENTIFYING AN ASSUMPTION

Page 6

1   **C is correct.** For Talia's conclusion to hold, it must be assumed that students must not do anything to hurt the reputation of the school: If Ramesh and Talia misbehave on the bus, it will hurt the school's reputation + students must not do anything to hurt the reputation of the school means therefore Ramesh and Talia must behave on the bus.

A is incorrect. This does not link the evidence to Talia's conclusion so it is not the assumption she made: If Ramesh and Talia misbehave on the bus, it will hurt the school's reputation + students from Ramesh and Talia's school often catch the bus **does not mean** Ramesh and Talia must behave on the bus.

B is incorrect. This is Talia's conclusion, not the missing assumption.

D is incorrect. This is the evidence Talia used to draw her conclusion.

2   **A is correct.** Ms Small's conclusion is that the Sea Life Aquarium should not be closed. She based this conclusion on the evidence that if the Sea Life Aquarium closes, it will hurt the local tourist economy. So for her conclusion to hold, it must be assumed that we should not do something that will hurt the local tourist economy: If the Sea Life Aquarium closes, it will hurt the local tourist economy + we should not do something that will hurt the local tourist economy means the Sea Life Aquarium should not be closed.

B is incorrect. This is Ms Small's conclusion.

C is incorrect. This is the evidence Ms Small used to draw her conclusion.

D is incorrect. This might be the real reason Ms Small does not want the Aquarium to close but it does not link the evidence to Ms Small's conclusion. Therefore it is not the assumption she made based on that evidence.

ANALYSNG REASONING TO JUDGE IF IT IS CORRECT

Page 7

1   **A is correct.** The information in the box tells you that anyone not interested in current affairs cannot become a successful newsreader so Emma's reasoning is correct. The information in the box does not tell you that anyone who is confident and interested in current affairs will certainly become a successful newsreader. Therefore Samesh's reasoning **is incorrect.**

2   **C is correct.** Since the pygmy possum is Australia's only hibernating marsupial, it must be the case that any possum that isn't a pygmy possum can't be hibernating. Hannah's statement uses correct reasoning. Since the pygmy possum is Australia's only hibernating marsupial then any marsupial that is definitely hibernating must be a pygmy possum. Rowan's reasoning is correct.

The other options are incorrect by a process of elimination.

IDENTIFYING FLAWED REASONING

Page 9

1   **C is correct.** To come to the conclusion that four entrants will get ribbons, Krystal has added the one ribbon for People's Choice to the three ribbons for first, second and third. She has then assumed the four ribbons will go to four different poets. She has not considered that the People's Choice winner might also come first, second or third—and therefore will receive two of the ribbons, meaning only three poets might get ribbons.

A is incorrect. The information in the box tells us each entrant can only enter one poem. So this sentence shows a mistake but it is not a mistake Krystal has made.

B and D are incorrect. These statements might be true but they do not impact the number of ribbons awarded and they are not mistakes Krystal has made.

2 **B is correct.** Darren assumes that since four competitions were won by students at his school during the year, there were four students who won those competitions. However, it may be that some students won more than one competition. In this case fewer than half of the qualifiers could be competition winners. So this statement shows the flaw in Darren's reasoning.

The other options are incorrect. These statements are irrelevant to Darren's claim and are not mistakes he has made.

IDENTIFYING ADDITIONAL EVIDENCE THAT STRENGTHENS A CLAIM
Page 11

1 **D is correct.** The claim the writer wants you to accept is that research into hibernation could be helpful for humans in fighting disease. The statement that most strengthens this argument is that recent studies on hibernation have led researchers to believe a major breakthrough in hibernation research is likely.

A is incorrect. This statement rephrases something already stated.

B is incorrect. This statement adds extra information about animal hibernation but does not strengthen the argument about human hibernation's potential for medical purposes.

C is incorrect. This statement documents an incident of human hibernation but does not strengthen the argument about medical hibernation for curing disease.

2 **C is correct.** The claim made by the spokesperson is that food packs distributed by charities prevent malnutrition in children when adequate nutritious food is unavailable. The statement that malnutrition negatively affects children's physical and mental development provides a reason to prevent malnutrition and

therefore strengthens the argument to provide food packs.

A is incorrect. The fact that peanut paste is nutrient rich is already stated in the text.

B is incorrect. This is additional information to that provided in the text but it does not strengthen the claim.

D is incorrect. This information is already provided in the text.

IDENTIFYING EVIDENCE THAT WEAKENS AN ARGUMENT
Page 13

1 **A is correct.** The manager claims that supplying fruit would be of little value to staff, yet 90% of staff are in favour of replacing biscuits with fruit. So this statement contradicts, and therefore weakens, the manager's claim.

B is incorrect. The manager could use this statement to strengthen the claim. It therefore does not weaken it.

C is incorrect. This statement neither strengthens nor weakens the claim.

D is incorrect. The manager has already mentioned this so this statement neither strengthens nor weakens the claim.

2 **D is correct.** Lucas claims they should not go swimming because it is too cold to swim. The statement that swimming in cold water improves your fitness and endurance because your heart must pump faster **most** weakens this claim because it undermines or limits the scope of the claim. If swimming in cold water is good for you, then the fact that it is cold does not hold up as a reason not to go swimming.

A is incorrect. This statement could weaken a general argument against going swimming but it does not weaken Lucas's claim that the water will be too cold to go swimming.

B is incorrect. This statement strengthens Charlotte's argument in favour of going swimming so they can relax. However, it does not weaken Lucas's claim that the water will be too cold to go swimming.

C is incorrect. This statement neither strengthens nor weakens Lucas's claim that the water will be too cold to go swimming.

IDENTIFYING AN ARGUMENT WITH THE SAME STRUCTURE

Page 15

1 **D is correct.** The argument introduces the topic of climate change and provides four problems it causes. Then it ends with a strong assertion about the need to address climate change. D introduces the topic of Fair Trade and provides four issues that Fair Trade addresses. Then it ends with a strong statement that Fair Trade should be supported.

A is incorrect. It makes an assertion ('It's easy to recycle at least 95% of household waste') and gives two conditions which impact your ability to recycle: you have to separate materials and you have to investigate local recycling options. This is a different structure to the argument in the box.

B is incorrect. It begins with a strong claim and then makes a strong recommendation. It does not have the same structure as the argument in the box.

C is incorrect. It makes a strong claim or assertion and gives two reasons to support the assertion. It does not conclude with a restatement of the claim.

2 **C is correct.** The argument Maggie wants you to accept is that the RSPCA does a great job rescuing injured animals. The supporting evidence is the information about the rescue of the sugar glider. In the final sentence Maggie restates the claim that the RSPCA does a great job rescuing injured animals. Sophie claims that the RSPCA does a great job in helping people and animals. She then provides evidence of how the RSPCA supports people and animals in relation to homelessness. Sophie ends by restating her claim.

A is incorrect because Chris makes a claim that baking a cake is a good way to support the RSPCA in fighting animal cruelty and gives evidence on the ways in which the money is used but does not restate the claim.

B is incorrect because Jonah provides information without making a claim or an assertion about the topic.

D is incorrect because Jamal makes a claim that training is important but gives no reason to support this claim.

USING VENN DIAGRAMS

Page 17

1 **B is correct.** Draw a simple Venn diagram. The rectangle holds all 12 guitar players. There are two overlapping circles to hold those who sing and those who play piano.

The 5 players who only play guitar go inside the rectangle but outside the circles. There are 7 people left but 5 sing and 5 play piano. This is $5 + 5 = 10$ choices. This means 3 people have been counted twice, as $10 - 7 = 3$. We can place the 3 people in the overlapping part of the circles as those who both sing and play piano.

B is correct. Three of the guitar players can also sing and play piano.

The completed Venn diagram is shown here. Five people sing, five play the piano and five only play guitar. Note that all numbers add to 12: the total number of guitarists.

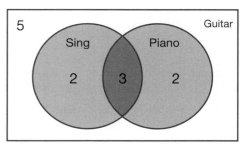

2 **C is correct.** Draw a simple Venn diagram. The rectangle holds all 22 players. Two overlapping circles will hold those who competed in swimming and athletics.

The 10 people who didn't compete in either go inside the rectangle but outside the circles.

$22 - 10 = 12$ so there are 12 people left to go inside the circles. 10 players competed in swimming. So there are 2 people left who competed in athletics but not swimming as $10 + 10 + 2 = 22$ players. Now there must be 10 inside the swimming circle but 5 of them competed **only** in swimming. Therefore the other 5 must have competed in both.

By adding the 5 who competed in both to the 2 that competed only in athletics, we have 7 players who competed in athletics.

C is correct. The completed Venn diagram is shown. Note that the numbers all add to 22, the total number of players on the team.

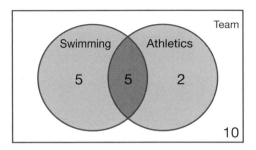

QUESTIONS WITH GRAPHS

Page 19

1   **B is correct.** Sector 2 is the largest and so must represent art. Sectors 1 and 5 are the same size so must represent sewing and metalwork. Sector 6 is exactly twice the size of sector 3 so must represent music and woodwork.

To see this we need to recognise that sector 4 is too large to be only half of sector 6 and is too small to be twice as large as sector 3. Therefore sector 4 cannot be music or woodwork. Sector 4 must be drama.

2   **D is correct.** The two statements should give us enough information to work out who is represented by each colour in the graph. We can then work out how many more goals Tony needed to kick to be the best.

If Barry kicked 8 out of 10 goals from one position, then he must be either the dark purple or the light purple, as the dark purple kicked 8 goals from position 2 and the light purple kicked 8 goals from position 3.

They each took 40 kicks and for Daisy half of them were goals. She must be the dark purple as it shows 5 + 8 + 3 + 4 = 20 goals kicked. So Barry must be the light purple and the white columns show Tony's kicks.

Barry's total is 5 + 7 + 8 + 1 = 21 goals. Tony's total is 7 + 5 + 5 + 2 = 19.

To have beaten Barry, Tony needed to have kicked an extra 3 goals. This would have taken his total to 19 + 3 = 22 goals.

DETERMINING THE DISTRIBUTION OF ITEMS

Page 21

1   **C is correct.** If 12 students didn't get any ice cream, then 28 students did: 40 – 12 = 28.

To find out how many students bought 2 scoops we find the difference between the number of scoops and the number of students who got ice cream.

Eight students got 2 scoops, as 36 – 28 = 8. This means the other 20 students got 1 scoop.

2   **B is correct.** If 22 chairs were empty, then 78 chairs were not empty: 100 – 22 = 78.

If 78 chairs took 113 people, then 35 chairs took 2 people: 113 – 78 = 35.

This means that 43 chairs took only 1 person, as 78 – 35 = 43.

SOLVING 2D PUZZLES

Page 22

1   **D is correct.** By pushing the shapes shown into position on the square, the outline of the shape needed is revealed. By rotating the shape in D by 180° you can see that it fits.

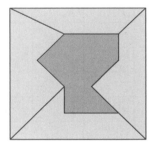

2   **B is correct.** The completed square is shown below.

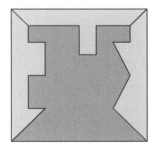

IDENTIFYING AND FOLLOWING A PATTERN Page 23

1 **B is correct.** The tiles along each diagonal from top left to bottom right are the same way up. By following this pattern we can see that B is the correct answer:

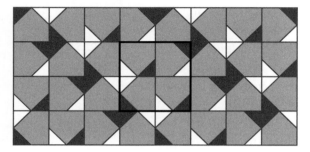

2 **A is correct.** In each row the arrows are either all pointing to a top corner or a bottom corner. In the fourth row down, all the arrows are pointing to a top corner. This leaves A and D as our options. The arrows in each row alternate between pointing to the top right and top left. This means A is our answer.

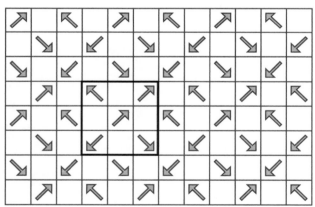

QUESTIONS INVOLVING FRACTIONS OF A QUANTITY Page 25

1 **C is correct.** The key to answering this question is to work out what fraction of the necklaces are represented by the 8 Carla sold in the first hour. To do this we must find out what fraction of the necklaces are sold during the other hours.

If $\frac{1}{2}$ and then $\frac{1}{4}$ of the necklaces are sold in the second and third hours, they represent $\frac{3}{4}$ of the necklaces, as:

$$\frac{1}{2} + \frac{1}{4} = \frac{2}{4} + \frac{1}{4} = \frac{3}{4}$$

This means 8 necklaces represent $\frac{1}{4}$ of the total, as:

$$1 - \frac{3}{4} = \frac{1}{4}$$

So if 8 necklaces represent one-quarter, Carla took $4 \times 8 = 32$ necklaces.

2 **B is correct.** To do this we need to work backwards from the last stop.

If half the people got off, leaving 6 people, then there must have been 12 people on the bus before stop C. Six people (half) got off and 6 people (half) stayed on.

Before stop B there must have been 15 people, as 3 people got off to leave 12 on the bus.

This means that after $\frac{1}{4}$ of the total passengers got off at stop A there were 15 passengers left. So 15 passengers represent $\frac{3}{4}$ of the number that were on the bus before stop A.

15 is $\frac{3}{4}$ of 20. So there were 20 people on the bus originally.

We could also go through the steps for each option. We can't start with 30 people because one-quarter can't get off as this won't be a whole number. Following the steps with 24 people won't work for a similar reason when we try to halve 15 people. 12 is too few people to start with. The only option that works is 20.

QUESTIONS ABOUT TIME DIFFERENCES Page 26

1 **D is correct.** Winnipeg is behind both of the other cities so it goes on the far left. La Paz is only 2 hours ahead so it comes next and Yakutsk is on the far right of the mini map. Yakutsk must be 13 hours ahead of La Paz.

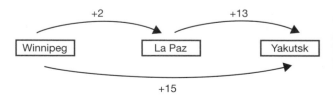

You must subtract 13 hours from the time in Yakutsk to get the time in La Paz.

You can do this in your head, remembering that you will go back into the previous day. Taking 13 hours from 11:45 am will get you to 10:45 pm the day before. So it is 10:45 pm on Tuesday.

2 A is correct. Look at the difference between the times given. Phoenix is behind Lima by 2 hours. Lima is behind Cairo by 7 hours. This means Phoenix is 9 hours behind Cairo. The mini map will look like this:

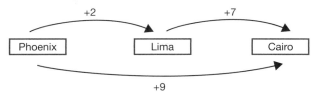

QUESTIONS INVOLVING RATES OF WORK
Page 27

1 B is correct. If 100 cranes are folded in 100 minutes, then they can fold 1 crane every minute, which is also 60 cranes in 60 minutes, or 60 cranes per hour. If Khaled folds 45 per hour, then Mansoor must fold the other 15 cranes, as 60 – 45 = 15 cranes. Mansoor folds 15 cranes per hour.

2 A is correct. Bryan baked 128 so Cassandra must have baked the other 72 cupcakes, as 200 – 128 = 72. They baked four batches over the 2 hours as each batch takes half an hour. So Cassandra can fit 18 cupcakes in her oven, as 72 ÷ 4 = 18.

FINDING THE BEST PRICE
Page 28

1 D is correct. To buy at least 8 biscuits, there are a few possibilities. Caleb can't buy two lots of 6 as he doesn't have $22. The best option, if he only needs 8 biscuits, is to buy one lot of 6 and 2 singles as $11 + $2.50 + $2.50 = $16. This means he gets $4 change.

2 A is correct. Even if we look at a number of weeks in a row, we only ever have a group of 3 days and a group of 2 days. A 7-day pass will cost $70. A 5-day pass ($52) and a 1-day pass ($15) will cost $67. The best combination is shown below.

Mon.	Tue.	Wed.	Thu.	Fri.	Sat.	Sun.
2-day		1-day		2-day		

The price for this is: 2 × $25 + $15 = $65.

DETERMINING DIFFERENT VIEWS OF 2D SHAPES
Page 29

1 D is correct. When looking at a 2D shape from the reverse side, it will appear as if the shape has been reflected. What is farthest to the left will now be farthest to the right. The two parts of the hill are the same height.

B is incorrect. The two parts of the hill are different heights.

A is incorrect. The hills have been reversed but the trees are still in the same places.

C is incorrect. A big tree is right on top of both hills, which is not the case in the original backdrop.

2 A is correct. The original card only has one semicircle on the top, so we can rule out B, as it has two. The far left end of D is not the exact reflection of the far right end from the original. The thin pointed part is also facing the wrong way. So we can rule out D. Similarly, those two parts of the card are wrong in option C.

SAMPLE TEST 1A

Page 31

1 C 2 A 3 C 4 B 5 C 6 D 7 A 8 B 9 C
10 A 11 B 12 B 13 C 14 A 15 B 16 D
17 B 18 A 19 D 20 B

1 If Cameron makes 8 of the 15 coffees in 10 minutes, then Ellie must make the other 7: 15 – 8 = 7. If Ellie makes 7 coffees in 10 minutes, she makes 7 × 6 = 42 coffees in 60 minutes.

2 Andreas has found a jacket that has a Torres Strait Islander flag on it and so it seems to match the description and he assumes it **must** be Maxi's. However, Andreas cannot say this with certainty. He has not thought that there might be other jackets with a Torres Strait Islander flag.

B is incorrect. Even if this is true, it is not a mistake Andreas has made.

C is incorrect. There is no information about the colour of the jacket the children are searching for and so this is not a mistake Andreas has made.

D is incorrect. Maxi has asked the children to search the lost property box so this is not a mistake Andreas has made.

3 Option C provides an example of how meat production harms the planet so it best supports Finn's claim that not eating meat is better for the planet.

A is incorrect. This could be one of the reasons Finn is trying not to eat meat but the statement does not support his claim that not eating meat is better for the planet.

B is incorrect. This statement does not support Finn's claim that not eating meat is better for the planet.

D is incorrect. This could be a reason to eat less meat but the statement does not support Finn's claim that not eating meat is better for the planet.

4 A 3-day pass ($60) is cheaper than three 1-day passes ($75) so should be used where possible. Five 1-day passes ($125) are more expensive than a 7-day pass ($120) so if there are 5 days inside a 7-day period, but no period of 3 consecutive days, then a 7-day pass is best.

By writing out the days of the month and underlining the days Kara needs we can see the best combination:

1 2 3 4 5 6 7 8 9 10 11 12 13 14 15

1-day   3-day   7-day

The cheapest combination is:
2 × $25 + $60 + $120 = $230.

5 Lucy's conclusion is that Toby's father has a good imagination. She has based this conclusion on the evidence that he is an author. So, for her conclusion to hold, it must be assumed that all authors have good imaginations: Toby's father is an author + all authors have good imaginations means therefore Toby's father has a good imagination.

A is incorrect. This assumption would not support Lucy's conclusion that Toby's father must have a good imagination.

B is incorrect. This is Lucy's conclusion, not her assumption.

D is incorrect. This is the evidence Lucy has used to base her conclusion on.

6 By pushing the shapes shown into position on the square, the outline of the shape needed is revealed.

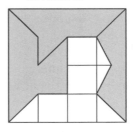 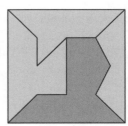

We can see that D will fit after a rotation.

7 The information given helps us work out which person is represented by which colour column in the graph.

If Killian scored the same on two of the quizzes, he must be either white or light purple. If Bernie scored the same as Killian in one of the tests, he must be dark purple and Killian must be white as they scored the same in the fourth quiz. Ivan must be the light purple.

Ivan's best score is 6 and his worst is 4. The difference between his best and worst scores is 6 – 4 = 2.

8 A cricket bat and bike are both included in the list of things Carlos wants to sell at the garage sale but neither Jim nor Lia has them to sell.

A is incorrect. Carlos does not want to sell a scooter or science kit.

C is incorrect. Carlos wants to sell a bike and some Lego bricks. However, both Jim and Lia have Lego bricks to sell.

D is incorrect. Carlos wants to sell some books and a cricket bat but Lia also wants to sell some books.

9 The main idea that Farid wants us to accept is that they should go to the pool this morning. The rest of the text gives more information about what they could do at the pool and after going to the pool.

A and D are incorrect. This is supporting information for the main idea.

B is incorrect. This information is not in the text so cannot be the main idea.

10 The total number of siblings is 28. If 10 students have 2 siblings, then those 10 students have 20 siblings in total. The rest of the students only have 0 or 1 sibling. As 28 – 20 = 8, there are 8 siblings of 8 of the students in the class. As 10 students have 2 siblings and 8 students have 1 sibling, 7 students have no siblings:

25 – 10 – 8 = 7.

11 From Mira and Lee's descriptions we know the fruit on the tree is orange, round and very small. So, based on the information in the box, it could be a cumquat tree. However, it could also be a mandarin tree with young, smaller fruit. So Mira is correct when she says it **might** be a mandarin tree and Lee is also correct when he says it **could** be a cumquat tree.

The other options are incorrect by a process of elimination.

12 The argument the writer wants you to accept is that it should not be necessary to automatically respect people who are older than you just because they are older. The argument that weakens the claim is the statement that says older people deserve a degree of respect because they must be wiser.

A is incorrect. This statement is irrelevant to the argument because it is about respect and obedience generally but not specific to automatically being required to respect older people who have not earned respect.

C and D are incorrect. These statements strengthen the argument.

13 If we look across the top row, we can see the dark corner of the tile starts in the top left, then in the next tile it is in the top right, then the bottom left, then the bottom right. The pattern then repeats. This is the same for every row except it is shifted one tile to the right.

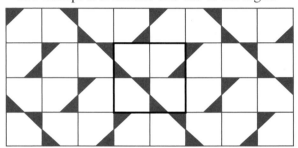

There are other ways to recognise a pattern in the tiles. Noticing that each diagonal from top left to bottom right includes tiles the same way up will also get you to the answer.

14 The information to consider is whether Dane read the class novel, whether he wrote the book review and whether it was possible for him to attend the author workshop and therefore be able to apply for a mentorship. It is not possible that Dane could attend the author workshop if he did not read the class novel because to attend the workshop students were required to submit a book review. **The other options are incorrect.** These sentences are all possible.

15 London is 3 hours ahead of Montevideo and 6 hours ahead of Chicago so Montevideo is 3 hours ahead of Chicago. A mini map of the time zones would look like this:

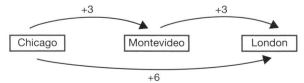

Add 3 hours to get from 4:20 pm in Chicago to 7:20 pm in Montevideo on the same day.

16 Isla has stamps from both China and Canada but neither Eric nor Cooper has stamps from these countries.

A is incorrect. Isla does not have stamps from India or South Korea.

B is incorrect. Isla has stamps from Australia and China but Cooper also has stamps from Australia.

C is incorrect. Isla has stamps from Canada and New Zealand but both Eric and Cooper also have stamps from New Zealand.

17 By pushing the shapes shown into position on the grid, the outline of the shape needed is revealed. By rotating the shape in B by 180° you can see that it fits.

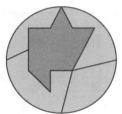

18 The main idea the creator of the text wants you to accept is that a new pedestrian and cycle bridge will be built at Black Lagoon. The rest of the text gives more information about the bridge to support that main idea.

B is incorrect. This background information is mentioned in the introductory sentence but it is not the main idea.

C is incorrect. This information is not in the text so it cannot be the main idea.

D is incorrect. This information is given in the text to support the main idea.

19 When a piece of paper is folded in half, the dotted lines are both lines of symmetry. This means the arrow must be mirrored in both lines. So the arrow in the top right must be a mirror image of the arrow in the top left. Also the bottom two arrows must be mirror images of the top two arrows. This is the case in D but no others.

20 To find the answer you must work backwards from $23. Before he spent $7 he had $23 + 7 = \$30$. Before his money was doubled he had $30 \div 2 = \$15$. Before he got $5 pocket money he had $15 - 5 = \$10$.

SAMPLE TEST 1B　Page 35

1 B　**2** B　**3** B　**4** A　**5** A　**6** B　**7** D　**8** B　**9** B
10 A　**11** D　**12** C　**13** A　**14** A　**15** A　**16** B
17 C　**18** D　**19** B　**20** D

1 The 2-day pass ($16) is cheaper than buying two 1-day passes ($20) so, where he can, Ahmad should buy 2-day passes to cover two consecutive days. The 5-day pass is $30, which is the same price, or more expensive, than 3 days covered by 1-day passes ($30) or a 2-day pass and a 1-day pass ($26). However, it is cheaper than any four-day combination. So if there are 4 days that can be covered by a 5-day pass, Ahmad should buy that. By writing out the days of the month and underlining the ones Ahmad wants, we can see the best combination below.

1 2 <u>3</u> 4 5 <u>6</u> <u>7</u> 8 <u>9</u> 10 11 12 13 <u>14</u> <u>15</u>
　　1-day　　2-day　1-day　　　　2-day

The price is: $2 \times 10 + 2 \times 16 = 20 + 32 = \$52$.

2 Noah says he will win a prize **for sure**. However, the information in the box states that completing the course and clearing at least 10 obstacles gives only a **chance** of winning a prize.

A is incorrect. This statement is irrelevant to winning a prize and is not a mistake Noah has made.

C and D are incorrect. These statements do not show a mistake Noah has made.

3 Together the team runs $20 + 6 + 14 = 40$ laps in 2 hours. There are four half hours in 2 hours so divide 40 by 4.

40 laps in 2 hours
$\div 2$　　$\div 2$
20 laps in 1 hour
$\div 2$　　$\div 2$
10 laps in half an hour

The team completed 10 laps in half an hour.

4 This statement gives another benefit of therapy dogs in schools so best supports Anya's claim that having therapy dogs in schools is a good idea.

B is incorrect. This does not support Anya's claim. In fact, it could weaken it.

C is incorrect. The fact that another school has a therapy dog does not mean it is a good idea to have one. So, on its own, this statement does not support Anya's claim.

D is incorrect. This statement does not support Anya's claim about therapy dogs being a good idea.

5 The completed square is shown below.

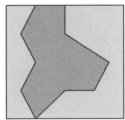

6 Draw a Venn diagram. The rectangle holds all students. Two overlapping circles hold the mobile owners and the computer owners.

The 3 students who don't own either go in the rectangle but outside the circles. This leaves 7 students to go inside the circles.

Four own mobiles and 5 own computers. This means there are $4 + 5 = 9$ people mentioned but only 7 people to fill the spots: $9 - 7 = 2$. This means 2 people have been counted twice so there must be 2 students who own both and must go in the overlapping part of the circles.

If 5 people own a computer but 2 of them own a mobile phone as well, then 3 students must own a computer and not a mobile phone.

The completed Venn diagram is shown below.

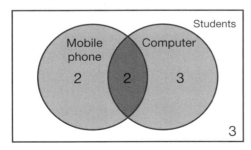

7 For the conclusion to hold, it must be assumed that fruit tasted better in the past: The fruit stall sells fruit that tastes like it did in the past + fruit tasted better in the past means therefore the fruit sold at the stall tastes better.

A is incorrect. This is the purpose of the advertisement.

B is incorrect. This is the evidence the writer has used to support the conclusion.

C is incorrect. This is the conclusion the writer has drawn.

8 To begin with we have 10 owners with 20 dogs. After we consider the owner with 5 dogs, there are 9 owners left with 15 dogs. After we consider the 2 owners with 3 dogs, there are 7 owners left with 9 dogs. These owners have either 1 or 2 dogs. To find out how many have 2 dogs, we can subtract the number of owners from the number of dogs. As $9 - 7 = 2$, there are 2 owners with 2 dogs and 5 owners that have only 1 dog.

9 The main idea the environmentalist wants us to accept is that Christmas Island is one of the top ten natural wonders of the world. The rest of the text gives more information about what makes the island a natural wonder of the world.

A is incorrect. This information is not in the text so cannot be the main idea.

C is incorrect. This is supporting information for the main idea.

D is incorrect. This could be the purpose of the environmentalist's speech but the information is not in the text so it cannot be the main idea.

10 The key to answering this question is to work out what fraction of the book is represented by the 15 pages he read on day 1. To do this we need to know how much of the book he read on the other days.

If $\frac{1}{3}$ and then $\frac{1}{6}$ of the pages are read on the second and third days, they represent $\frac{1}{2}$ of the book:

$$\frac{1}{3} + \frac{1}{6} = \frac{2}{6} + \frac{1}{6} = \frac{3}{6} = \frac{1}{2}$$

This means the 15 pages read on day 1 are half the book:

$$1 - \frac{1}{2} = \frac{1}{2}$$

So there are $15 \times 2 = 30$ pages in the book.

11 If Boston is 7 hours behind Kyiv, then Kyiv is 7 hours ahead of Boston. A mini map of the time zones would look like this:

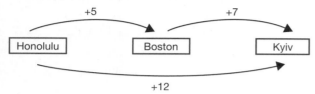

Kyiv is 12 hours ahead of Honolulu. So we must add 12 hours to the time in Honolulu. The time is 9:00 am the next day.

12 Mark's claim is that artificial intelligence is better for refereeing sporting matches than human referees because humans make mistakes and can be biased. The statement that weakens his claim is that referees sometimes need to adjudicate between players and AI won't be able to judge if human players are being truthful.

A is incorrect. This statement is irrelevant to the argument because a player's feelings are irrelevant to a referee.

B is incorrect. This statement is irrelevant because the argument is about whether AI is better than humans, not whether it is more expensive.

D is incorrect. This statement strengthens Mark's argument.

13 If Lachie does not give his mother a book, you can conclude he must have painted her a picture. Since he gives her a painting, he must also give her a candle.

B is incorrect. You can conclude that Lachie will only give his mum vouchers if he doesn't get her a candle.

C is incorrect. Lachie will give a candle OR some vouchers, not both.

D is incorrect. Lachie says that if he paints her a picture, he will also give her a candle.

14 B is incorrect. The spike in the middle is not symmetrical like in the original.

C is incorrect. The building on the far left is not the correct shape.

D is incorrect. The building on the far left is flipped incorrectly.

15 The argument is structured as follows: an introduction to the topic or definition of the argument, then reasons to support the argument and then a call to action. Option A has this structure. It introduces the Martuwarra Fitzroy River and provides reasons for its value. It concludes with a call to protect it.

B is incorrect. This argument introduces the river and provides information about its value.

C is incorrect. This argument begins with a call to action, then gives a reason to support the action.

D is incorrect. This argument introduces the topic by stating that the traditional owners of the Martuwarra Fitzroy River area oppose water extraction and then gives a reason for their opposition. It does not include a call to action.

16 Bangkok is the furthest behind so it goes on the left. Suva is ahead of the other cities so it goes 'on the right. The mini map should look like this:

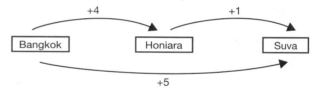

Honiara is 4 hours ahead of Bangkok so we subtract 4 hours from 3:00 pm in Honiara to get 11:00 am in Bangkok on the same day.

17 For this conclusion to hold, it must be assumed that helping the local economy is a good thing: Buying locally helps the local economy + helping the local economy is a good thing means therefore people should buy locally.

A is incorrect. This sentence does not link the evidence to the conclusion so it is not the assumption that has been made: Buying locally helps the local economy + there is a new local store near Wei's house does **not** mean people should buy locally.

B is incorrect. This is the conclusion, not the missing assumption.

D is incorrect. This is the evidence used to draw the conclusion.

18 If 5 courts **weren't** being used, then 45 courts **were** being used. If everyone was playing singles, then 90 people would be playing. However, there were 132 people so there were 132 – 90 = 42 extra people playing. These people can be shared out between the courts two at a time. This can be done 42 ÷ 2 = 21 times. So there were 21 courts playing doubles.

This means there were 45 – 21 = 24 courts playing singles. There were two people on each of those courts, so there were 48 people playing singles.

We can check this answer:

$$21 \times 4 + 24 \times 2 = 84 + 48$$
$$= 132$$

19 To come to the conclusion that four entrants will get prizes, Harper has added the one special prize to the three prizes for first, second and third. She has then assumed that the four prizes will go to four different entrants. She has not thought that the special prize winner might also come first, second or third—and therefore will receive two of the prizes. So it is possible for only three entrants to get prizes.

A and C are incorrect. These statements might be true but they do not impact the number of prizes and they are not mistakes Harper has made.

D is incorrect. The information tells us that each entrant can enter only one photograph. So this sentence shows a mistake but it is not a mistake Harper has made.

20 From the information you can draw the conclusion that if Thomas was tired at the audition, he would forget the lines and that if he forgets the lines, he does not stand a chance of getting the lead role. Therefore this conclusion cannot be true.

A is incorrect. This statement might be true. Even though Thomas stayed up late, he might not have been tired for the audition. The information tells us he will likely be tired, not that he will **definitely** be tired. If he isn't tired, he might still remember all the lines and be offered the lead role.

B is incorrect. This statement might be true. Even if he did not stay up late with Sara, Thomas might have still been tired and forgotten the lines. Or he might have forgotten the lines—and not been offered the role—even if he was not tired.

C is incorrect. This statement might be true. The information tells us that if Thomas remembers all the lines, he **might** be offered the role—not that he will **definitely** be offered it.

SAMPLE TEST 2A   Page 39

1 D **2** C **3** B **4** A **5** A **6** D **7** A **8** C **9** D **10** C **11** C **12** D **13** D **14** D **15** B **16** B **17** D **18** A **19** C **20** A

1 By pushing the shapes shown into position on the square, the outline of the shape needed is revealed.

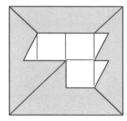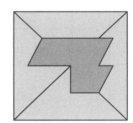

2 According to the instructor if a rider has less than 40 hours of riding practice, they don't have a chance of being moved up to the advanced class. Therefore none of the riders who have less than 40 hours of riding practice will be moved up to the advanced class.

A is incorrect. According to the instructor, having 40 hours of riding practice gives a rider only a **chance** of being moved up to the advanced class. It does not guarantee being moved up.

B is incorrect. The instructor says riders must have **at least** 40 hours of riding practice, not **less than** 40 hours of riding practice.

D is incorrect. The instructor says riders **must** have at least 40 hours of riding practice so this statement cannot be true.

3 Sam's conclusion is that the new teacher must be kind. He has based this conclusion on the evidence that the new teacher wears glasses. So, for his conclusion to hold, it must be assumed that all people who wear glasses are kind: The new teacher wears glasses + all people who wear glasses are kind means therefore the new teacher must be kind.

A is incorrect. This is Sam's conclusion, not his assumption.

C is incorrect. This is the evidence Sam has used to draw his conclusion.

D is incorrect. This assumption would not support Sam's conclusion.

4 The top row and the third row are the same. The second-top row and the fourth (bottom) row are the same. By looking at the top row and the bottom row we can work out which are the missing tiles. This is just one way of finding the pattern.

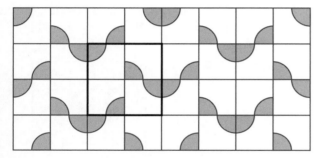

5 The vet wants the cat owner to accept the claim that Hairy Cat shampoo will improve the cat's fur quality and smell. The statement that most strengthens the vet's claim is that Hairy Cat has been designed by cat experts for optimum cat hairiness and a good aroma.

B is incorrect. This statement provides additional evidence to support the vet's claim but it only addresses one aspect—the poor fur quality—and not the issue of the smell so this is not the most supportive statement.

C is incorrect. This statement might be true but it does not support the argument to buy Hairy Cat for the Devon Rex.

D is incorrect. The fact that the vet gets a commission on each bottle of Hairy Cat sold and donates that money to the animal shelter might be an additional reason to buy the shampoo but it is not the most supportive statement for the claim that Hairy Cat will improve the cat's fur quality and smell.

6 If Heidi and Louisa scored the same at one of the positions, then they are the dark-purple and medium-purple columns as they both scored the same at Position 4.

Charissa and Louisa scored the same overall. The striped total is 7 + 8 + 4 + 5 = 24 and the medium purple total is 4 + 6 + 8 + 6 = 24.

Louisa must therefore be the medium purple and Heidi must be the dark purple. Heidi's total is 3 + 4 + 5 + 6 = 18 and one-third of 18 is 6. Heidi scored 6 from position 4.

7 If he sells 10 students pack C, that is 10 × 3 = 30 portraits. There are now 80 packs left comprising 135 portraits. To find how many students bought 2 portraits (pack B), we subtract the number of packs from the number of portraits: 135 − 80 = 55.

So 10 students get pack C (3 photos) and 55 students get pack B (2 photos). That is 65 packs out of 90, which means there are 25 packs left that have 1 photo (pack A).

8 Zac's argument is that libraries should be closed because they are unnecessary when people can borrow books online. The statement which most weakens his argument is that libraries are community centres.

A is incorrect. This statement could be true but it does not weaken Zac's argument because the statement applies to all books, digital and printed.

B is incorrect. This statement is true but it does not weaken Zac's argument.

D is incorrect. This statement is true but it is not expressed in a way that weakens Zac's argument.

9 Noah's reasoning is incorrect. He cannot declare that Monty **will** win. Monty might have a chance of winning but Noah needs to acknowledge that other dogs in the competition could also show all the characteristics that Yusuf believes will make Monty a winner. It will all depend which dog is best on the day.

A is incorrect. Arabella is correct that even if Monty is all the things Yusuf says he is, he may not win the competition.

B is incorrect. Paris is correct in recognising that Yusuf is biased towards his own dog.

C is incorrect. Yusuf expresses the opinion that he would award Monty the prize. His reasoning is correct because he is only speaking for himself and not declaring that Monty **will** win based on the judges' decision.

10 The key to answering this question is to find out what fraction of buildings is represented by the seven that have three storeys. To do this we need to know what fraction the other buildings make up.

If $\frac{1}{2}$ and $\frac{1}{3}$ of the buildings are single or double storey, they make up $\frac{5}{6}$ of the buildings:

$$\frac{1}{2} + \frac{1}{3} = \frac{3}{6} + \frac{2}{6} = \frac{5}{6}$$

This means the remaining seven buildings make up $\frac{1}{6}$ of the total:

$$1 - \frac{5}{6} = \frac{1}{6}$$

So there are $6 \times 7 = 42$ buildings in the street.

11 Both Sage and Greg show correct reasoning.

Since you need to have good spatial awareness to become a successful tiler, Sage is correct to reason that Eddie would 'likely not be a successful tiler because he does not have great spatial awareness'.

Greg uses correct reasoning when he says that Mollie could be a successful tiler if she decided she wanted to be one because she shows great attention to detail and good spatial awareness.

The other answers are incorrect by a process of elimination.

12 The main idea the expert wants us to accept is that mosquitoes are the deadliest creatures on earth. The rest of the text gives more information about why mosquitoes are so deadly.

A and B are incorrect. This is supporting information for the main idea.

C is incorrect. This could be the purpose of the expert's speech but the information is not in the text so it cannot be the main idea.

13 Dublin is behind the other two cities so it goes at the far left of the mini map. Auckland goes on the far right as it is the furthest ahead. Adding the 8 hours between Dublin and Perth and the 5 hours between Perth and Auckland

shows us that Auckland is 13 hours ahead of Dublin.

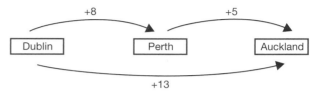

Add 13 hours to 4:15 pm and we get 5:15 am on the next day.

14 If Jarrod did not order enough tiles, he would not have been able to complete the job and it would not have been possible for him to get a bonus payment.

A is incorrect. Even if Jarrod did not measure the floor accurately, he could still have ordered enough tiles.

B is incorrect. He might not have completed the job on time.

C is incorrect. Jarrod could have completed the job on time but still not been given a bonus payment.

15 Together they earn $17 + 11 + 8 = \$36$ per hour. How many lots of 36 do we need to fit into \$90?

36 goes into 90 two and a half times. So they will earn the \$90 in $2\frac{1}{2}$ hours.

$36 in 1 hour
$\div 2 \quad \div 2$
$18 in a half hour
$\times 5 \quad \times 5$
$90 in 2.5 hours

16 Only Arshan's reasoning is correct. Since Ms Flint always wears the team colours to school on Monday if the team won a game on the weekend; today is Monday; and she is not wearing the team colours, then the team cannot have won a game on the weekend.

A is incorrect. Louise's reasoning has a flaw. Just because Ms Flint wears the team colours if the team wins, it does not follow that she does not wear the team colours at any other time. So it is possible that Ms Flint wore the team colours even though her team did not win a game on the weekend and Louise cannot say that the team **must** have won.

C and D are incorrect by a process of elimination.

17 The last bit of information tells us there are twice as many mammals as reptiles. This means sector 5 must be mammals and reptiles must be sectors 3 or 4. This is because sector 5 is exactly twice as big as sectors 3 or 4.

There are more birds than mammals, which means that sector 2 must be birds as it is the only sector larger than sector 5.

There are fewer amphibians than fish so sector 1 must be the amphibians and fish must be one of sectors 3 and 4.

Sectors 3 and 4 represent reptiles and fish.

18 Samir's mother's argument is that by building the new house the family will be able to rely totally on solar energy. The statement that the solar panels will be expandable supports this argument and counters Samir's claim that they won't be able to charge their electronic devices in the new house. Therefore it most strengthens Samir's mother's argument.

B is incorrect. This statement weakens Samir's mother's argument.

C is incorrect. This statement strengthens the argument about being able to rely on solar power but it does not counter Samir's claim. Therefore it does not **most** strengthen the argument.

D is incorrect. This statement supports a general argument in favour of building a more sustainable house but it is irrelevant to the argument about solar power.

19 Taking away the 2 days he wore neither spots nor stripes, there are 8 days left. But we know that on 7 of them he wore stripes and on 4 of them he wore spots. There are 7 + 4 = 11 days mentioned for only 8 possible days. That means 3 days are counted twice, as 11 − 8 = 3.

So these must be the days when he wears both spots and stripes.

20 By pushing the shapes shown into position on the square, the outline of the shape needed is revealed.

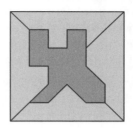

SAMPLE TEST 2B   Page 44

1 C **2** B **3** B **4** B **5** A **6** B **7** D **8** A **9** D
10 C **11** C **12** B **13** C **14** D **15** D **16** A
17 C **18** C **19** D **20** B

1 If Mr Young had double $38, he would have $76 to spend. He could have bought a 6-kg pack ($50) and two 1-kg ($24) packs for a total of $74. This is 8 kg of cherries. So, by doubling the amount he can spend, Mr Young can get an extra 4.5 kg of cherries.

2 Dimitri's argument is that all players in a team deserve the same salary because they are all equally responsible for team wins and losses. B is the statement that most weakens Dimitri's argument because it acknowledges that some players have more talent and therefore deserve more pay than others in the team.

A is incorrect. This statement strengthens the argument to pay team members equally.

C is incorrect. This statement strengthens the argument that players should be paid according to their talent and weakens Dimitri's argument that all team members deserve equal pay but it is not as strong an argument as B.

D is incorrect. The argument that some clubs cannot afford to attract star players with offers of high salaries strengthens Dimitri's argument rather than weakens it.

3 Together they can lay 57 + 44 + 19 = 120 pavers in an hour. This is 20 pavers every 10 minutes:

120 pavers in 60 minutes
÷ 6   ÷ 6
20 pavers in 10 minutes
× 5   × 5
100 pavers in 50 minutes

So in 50 minutes they will have laid 100 pavers.

4 From the information given, anyone who likes yoga likes Pilates and (since they like Pilates) they also like spin but not crossfit. It is therefore impossible for someone who likes yoga to like crossfit so B must be true.

The other answers are incorrect. These statements cannot be true.

5 If 7 picked batting and 6 picked bowling, then there are 7 + 6 = 13 choices made but there are only 11 people on the cricket team. 13 − 11 = 2. So 2 people were counted twice, meaning they liked both batting and bowling.

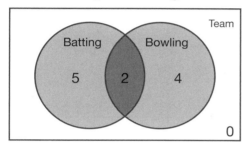

6 Skye's scores must be represented by the striped columns as her score gets lower each term until the last term. Brock's scores must be represented by the dark purple as they get better every term until the last term. This means Abby's scores are shown in light purple. Her best score is 14 in Term 2 and her worst score is 8 in Term 4: 14 − 8 = 6.

7 Based on the information provided it is not possible that Fish got a treat if he did not go on an evening walk.

A is incorrect. It is possible that Fish was worn out and got a treat. The information tells you that if Fish is worn out, he does not have a hope of getting a treat on his evening walk.

B is incorrect. It is possible that Fish walked well in the evening but did not get a treat. The information tells you that if Fish is cooperative on his evening walk, he **might** get a treat. It doesn't state that he **will** get a treat.

C is incorrect. It is possible that Fish walked well at midday but did not go for an evening walk.

8 To begin with there are 143 owners with 180 cars. After we consider the 10 owners with 3 cars each, there are 133 owners (143 − 10 = 133)

with 150 cars (180 − 3 × 10 = 150). After we consider the 45 owners with 2 cars each, there are 88 owners (133 − 45 = 88) with 60 cars (150 − 2 × 45 = 60). This means 60 owners have 1 car each and 28 have no cars at all.

9 The main idea of the text is that Teff is an important crop for Ethiopia. All of the information provided supports or expands on the idea that teff is important for farmers' incomes, as food for Ethiopian people, as a sustainable crop and as an energy-efficient crop.

A and B are incorrect. These statements reinforce the idea that teff is an important food source but neither statement covers the fact that teff is an important crop for farmers and so neither statement is the main idea of the text.

C is incorrect. This statement provides additional information about teff's sustainability as a food crop in a dry climate but this is not the main idea of the text.

10 Douglas has assumed that because three people qualified by winning an international event during the previous ten years, this means three of the qualifiers must have qualified by winning two regional events each during the year. However, some of the poets who qualified may have won more than two regional events and also competed at an international event.

The other options are incorrect. These statements are not mistakes Douglas has made.

11 The completed solution is shown below.

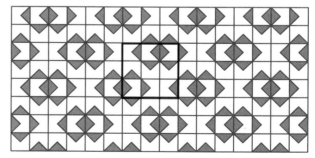

12 Start with 34 guests, then take 10 away to get 24 guests. One-third of these guests then leave. One-third of 24 is 8. So 8 guests leave. There are now 24 − 8 = 16 guests left at the party.

13 Since everyone had to vote for two of the three charities, knowing that no student voted for both the Cancer Council and the animal hospital tells you that everyone must have voted for UNICEF. C is the option that allows you to determine which charity won the vote. The outcome will be to donate to UNICEF.

The other options are incorrect. They do not lead you to this conclusion.

14 A is incorrect. The large mountain in the middle has not been flipped and is out of shape.

B is incorrect. The first valley on the left is too deep.

C is incorrect. The valley on the far right is too deep.

15 If the person who washed the car needed the time and the car key and Django had both, then he might have been the one who washed the car.

A is incorrect. Just because he had the time and the car key, it does not mean that Django must have washed the car. It only means he might have.

B is incorrect. It's true that Django can't have washed the car if he did not have the key but there may have been other reasons why he did not wash the car.

C is incorrect. It's true that Django can't have washed the car if he did not have the time but there may have been other reasons why Django did not wash the car.

16 The oval shape and the shape that looks like mountains are facing the wrong way. All other options can be rotated to look like the reverse side.

17 The writer of the argument in the box wants us to accept that we need to look after old trees and natural hollows. The writer begins by providing evidence about old trees, natural hollows and their importance, and concludes with the claim that we need to look after them. Option C uses this same structure. It begins by providing evidence about nest boxes in general and then Aussie Nest Boxes specifically, and concludes with the claim that Aussie Nest Boxes are the best choice to help wildlife.

A is incorrect. This text is informative and does not have an argument structure.

B is incorrect. This text begins by stating a claim (nest boxes must be monitored) and follows this with reasons to support this claim.

D is incorrect. The writer of this text does not want us to use rat poison or slug baits. However, the text is structured as an instruction (telling us what to do or not to do) rather than an argument.

18 Draw a simple Venn diagram. The rectangle holds all 15 chocolate bars. Two overlapping circles will hold the ones with caramel and those with nougat.

The 3 bars that have no caramel or nougat go outside the circles but inside the rectangle. This leaves 15 − 3 = 12 bars left to go inside the circles.

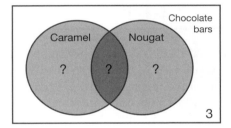

We are told that 10 have caramel and 8 have nougat. This is 10 + 8 = 18 bars to fill 12 spots inside the circles. So 6 bars are counted twice, as 18 − 12 = 6. Six bars go inside the overlapping part of the circle.

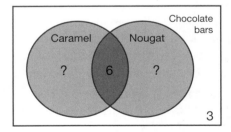

So of the 10 bars that have caramel, 6 bars have nougat as well, leaving 4 bars that have caramel but not nougat.

The complete Venn diagram is shown below.

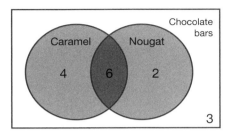

19 According to the teacher if a student has not read for at least 20 minutes at least five times a week, then they do not have a chance of winning a prize. Therefore none of the students who have read for less than 20 minutes five times a week will win a prize. So statement D must be true.

A is incorrect. According to the teacher, reading for 20 minutes five times a week gives a student only a **chance** of winning a prize. It does not guarantee a prize.

B is incorrect. This is the minimum required to have a **chance** of winning a prize. It does not guarantee a prize and students who have read more also have a **chance** of winning a prize.

C is incorrect. The teacher says students **must** have read for at least 20 minutes at least five times a week so if a student has read for less than 20 minutes, they cannot win a prize even if they have read more than five times during the week.

20 Ying's conclusion is that there is nothing wrong with staying up late on a school night. She has based this conclusion on the evidence that all her friends do. So for her conclusion to hold, it must be assumed that it is okay to do something if all your friends do it: All my friends stay up late on a school night + it's okay to do something if all your friends do it means therefore there's nothing wrong with staying up late on a school night.

A is incorrect. This is Ying's conclusion, not her assumption.

C is incorrect. This is the evidence Ying has used to base her conclusion on.

D is incorrect. This assumption does not support Ying's conclusion.

SAMPLE TEST 3A

Page 49

1 D **2** A **3** B **4** C **5** C **6** C **7** A **8** A **9** A
10 B **11** C **12** D **13** C **14** D **15** A **16** A
17 C **18** D **19** B **20** D

1 The completed square is shown below.

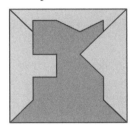

2 The argument is that berries are too expensive for people to eat as often as recommended by nutritionists and so should be subsidised by governments. Option A strengthens this argument by providing additional supportive information.

B is incorrect. This weakens the argument because it details the impracticality of subsidising berries.

C is incorrect. This statement weakens the argument by claiming it would never get public approval.

D is incorrect. This information is already provided in the text and so does not strengthen the argument.

3 From the information given, anyone who likes succulents likes cacti and (since they like cacti) they also like banksia but not roses. It is therefore not possible for someone who likes succulents to like roses so B must be true.

The other options are incorrect. These statements cannot be true.

4 Each square of four tiles on the floor includes all four possible ways to place the tile. That is, if we look at each purple section as an arrow, they point in four different directions. In the second and third row, each square of four tiles shows the arrows pointing in an anticlockwise direction. Option C continues this pattern.

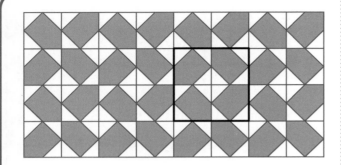

5   The argument the writer wants you to accept is that action to address climate change is a matter of urgency. The evidence provided to support this main idea is that coral cannot survive bleaching and acidification of the ocean and coral is essential for the survival of one million other species.

   A is incorrect. This statement is additional information and therefore not the main idea of the text.

   B is incorrect. This evidence to support the main idea is implied in the text in the argument that coral reefs support one million other species. It is not the main idea in the text.

   D is incorrect. This is the introduction to the argument and the evidence but the main idea is the call to action at the end of the argument.

6   If the person who ate all the chocolates and left the empty wrappers in the box must have had both an opportunity and a motive, then anyone who did not have both an opportunity and a motive cannot have been the person who ate them.

   The other options are incorrect. Each of these sentences shows incorrect reasoning.

7   Draw a simple Venn diagram. The rectangle holds all 8 students. Two overlapping circles will hold the numbers of students that like soccer and basketball.

   The 2 students who like neither sport go outside the circles but inside the rectangle. This leaves 8 – 2 = 6 students left to go inside the circles.

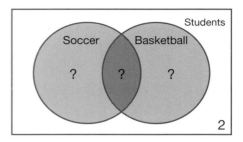

We are told that 5 like soccer and 5 like basketball. This is 10 students to fill 6 spots inside the circles. So 4 students are counted twice, as 10 – 6 = 4. Four students go inside the overlapping part of the circle.

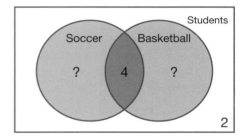

So, of the 5 students who like soccer, 4 like basketball as well, leaving 1 student who likes soccer but not basketball.

The complete Venn diagram is shown below.

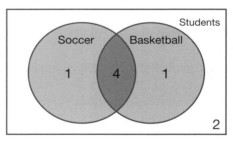

8   If 108 were carrying only one passenger, then there were 310 – 108 = 202 people left to be taken. They must be in pairs on the tuk-tuks. This means they are on 202 ÷ 2 = 101 tuk-tuks. So 108 tuk-tuks were carrying one person and 101 were carrying two people. 108 + 101 = 209 tuk-tuks with passengers.

   This leaves 11 tuk-tuks that were empty.

9   Lana's argument is that the majority of students have no need for maths beyond Year 6. Her argument is contradicted by option A which states that educational institutions often require some level of maths for entry to any

course, meaning it would be a disadvantage not to study maths in high school.

C and B are incorrect. These statements support Lana's argument.

D is incorrect. This statement neither supports nor contradicts Lana's argument.

10 We must find out what fraction of the guests is represented by the 15 who arrived late. To do this we need to know what fraction the other guests make.

If $\frac{1}{4}$ and then $\frac{1}{8}$ arrived on time or early, then they make up $\frac{3}{8}$ of the total number of guests:

$$\frac{1}{4} + \frac{1}{8} = \frac{2}{8} + \frac{1}{8} = \frac{3}{8}$$

So the 15 guests must represent the other $\frac{5}{8}$ of the total number of guests:

$$1 - \frac{3}{8} = \frac{5}{8}$$

If $\frac{5}{8}$ of the total is 15, then $\frac{1}{8}$ is 3, as $15 \div 5 = 3$. This means the total number of guests is $8 \times 3 = 24$.

11 The structure of the argument in the box is that the speaker, Rose, chooses one option over another option and gives two reasons for her choice. Rose chooses soccer over hockey and gives two reasons: the difficulty of hitting the hockey ball with the hockey stick and her lack of coordination. In option C, Eric chooses dark chocolate over milk chocolate and gives two reasons to support his choice: it isn't as sweet and it's good for you.

The other options are incorrect. These arguments express a preference of one choice over another but only give one reason for that choice.

12 Since everyone had to vote for two of the three venues, knowing that no student voted for both Burger Basement and Sushi Central tells you that everyone must have voted for Pizza Palace. D is the statement that allows you to work out the result of the vote: that the team will go to Pizza Palace for the end-of-season party. Other options cannot help you work out which venue was chosen.

13 Montreal is behind the other cities so is situated at the far left of the mini map. Reykjavik is ahead so it goes on the far right. The mini map should look like this:

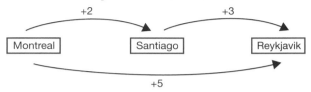

Reykjavik is 3 hours ahead of Santiago so we add 3 hours onto 10:00 am. This time is 1:00 pm on the same day.

14 Timmy's reasoning is correct. If the scores in writing were different but the scores in reading were the same, then they could not have got equal marks for English so Timmy's statement must be true.

Jess's reasoning is correct. If the scores in writing were the same but the scores in reading were different, then they would not have had equal marks so Jess's statement is true.

The other options are incorrect by a process of elimination.

15 The cheapest option to get 750 games over three months is to buy 500 games ($80), two lots of 100 games ($36) and one lot of 50 games ($10). This comes to $126.

At first he paid $50 per month, which is $150 over three months.

$$150 - 126 = \$24$$

He will save $24 over three months.

16 We know that any students who did not have a chance to perform in last term's play **will** be offered a part in this term's play. However, this does not mean that anyone who had a part in last term's play will definitely **not** be offered a part again this term. Therefore option A shows the flaw in Noah's reasoning and he may be offered a part again this term.

B is incorrect. This sentence is true and is not a mistake Noah has made.

C is incorrect. This sentence is a mistake since Noah's teacher said they definitely will be offered a part this term. However, it is not a mistake made by Noah.

D is incorrect. This sentence is true and is not a mistake Noah has made.

17 The graph is split into parts that are grouped together as 1 dark purple, 4 white, 2 light purple and 5 spotted parts. If Carlos owns twice as many coins from Asia as from Africa, and twice as many coins from South America (20) as from Asia (10), then South America is the white, Asia is the light purple and Africa is the dark purple, as these colours represent 4, 2 and 1 parts. The spotted rectangles must represent Europe.

If the 2 parts for Asia represent 10 coins, then each part represents 5 coins. Europe is five parts. Therefore Carlos has $5 \times 5 = 25$ coins from Europe.

The completed graph looks like this:

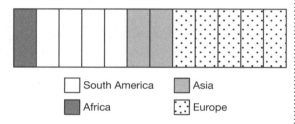

| | South America | | Asia |
| | Africa | | Europe |

Each small rectangular section represents 5 coins.

18 Mo claims a wildlife crossing is needed above Forest Road to connect the bushland reserves on either side. He supports this claim by saying the crossing is needed to protect wildlife so they are not forced to the ground. The statement about tree-top species being in more danger when they are forced to the ground to cross the road best supports his claim.

A and B are incorrect. These statements do not support Mo's claim that a crossing is needed above the road.

C is incorrect. This statement tells what Mo is going to do but does not **best** support his claim that the crossing is needed.

19 We need to find out who could have the largest shoe size.

From the first and third statements, we see that Nathaniel has a smaller shoe size than Quinn and Peter has a smaller shoe size than Quinn. This is not enough information to tell who has the largest shoe but it must be Quinn or Olivia.

Which of these two could be the shortest?

The fourth statement tells us that Quinn is taller than Olivia so he cannot be the shortest. Only Olivia can be the shortest but also have the largest shoe size.

(This question could be solved just as well by finding that Olivia and Peter could be the shortest but that only Olivia could have the largest shoe size.)

20 In D, the paper has been folded in half four times. This could have been done in a couple of different ways but definitely using four folds. While the other pieces are all different, they can all be made by folding in half three times exactly.

SAMPLE TEST 3B Page 54

1 A **2** D **3** D **4** B **5** A **6** C **7** B **8** C **9** C
10 C **11** D **12** B **13** D **14** C **15** A **16** C
17 B **18** A **19** A **20** C

1 With the first Monday being day 1, write out the 14 days and underline the days needed. Work out which deals are best.

An 8-day and 5-day pass would cover the whole time for a cost of $950, as $400 + 550 = 950$. However, the 5-day pass only covers three days of use. As this pass costs $400, and a 1-day pass costs $120, it would be cheaper to use three 1-day passes. Further still, a 2-day pass is cheaper than two 1-day passes so anywhere we can cover two days with a 2-day pass we should. The best option is shown below.

1 2 3 4 5 6 7 8 9 10 11 12 13 14
2-day   8-day   1-day

The price is $200 + $550 + $120 = $870.

Using a combination of two 2-day and four 1-day passes would get us a very close second at $880.

2 Neither Ria nor Max's reasoning is correct.

A is incorrect. Ria reasons that because the animal is on land and has four flippers it **must** be a sea lion. Her reasoning is incorrect. The information tells us that both sea lions and seals spend time on the land. Also she cannot say with certainty that it is a sea lion because it has four flippers, since there is nothing in the information stating that seals do not have four flippers.

B is incorrect. Max reasons that because the animal is on its belly, it **must** be a seal. His reasoning is incorrect since he hasn't thought that it could be a sea lion resting on its belly. For Max to reason that it **must** be a seal, he would need to say it is wriggling on its belly to move on land.

C is incorrect. Neither Ria nor Max's reasoning is correct.

3 The completed square is shown below.

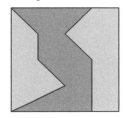

4 This statement provides a reason why students working in the garden should wear gardening gloves so it best supports the teacher's claim.

A is incorrect. This statement says that gloves are available but does not provide a reason to support the claim that students should wear the gloves.

C and D are incorrect. These statements do not provide a reason to support the claim that students should wear gloves while they are working in the garden.

5 Draw a simple Venn diagram. The rectangle holds all 20 flags. Two overlapping circles will hold the red and blue flags.

The 4 flags that have no red or blue go outside the circles but inside the rectangle.

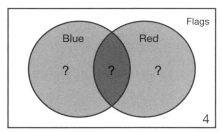

This means 20 − 4 = 16 flags must go inside the two circles. The information in the questions tells us that 14 have blue and 10 have red. This is 14 + 10 = 24 flags mentioned but there are only 16 flags. 24 − 16 = 8. This means that 8 flags have been counted twice. Write 8 inside the overlapping section of the circles.

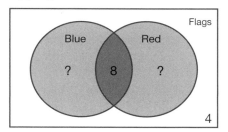

If 10 flags have red, then 10 − 8 = 2 flags have red but don't have blue. The answer is A.

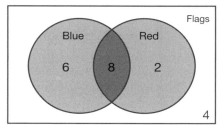

6 Sector 1 is the only sector bigger than a quarter circle so it must represent the oval. Sectors 3 and 5 are the only two sectors equal in size so they must represent the sandpit and the handball courts.

Together sectors 3 and 4 (or sectors 4 and 5) make up exactly one-quarter of the circle so sector 4 must be the basketball courts. This leaves sectors 2 and 6 to represent the library and the play equipment. As more people play in the library, it must be sector 6 and the play equipment must be sector 2.

7 The main idea that the creator of the text wants you to accept is that Southside sports field has been upgraded. The rest of the text supports this main idea by giving more information about the upgrade.

A is incorrect. This background supporting information is mentioned in the introductory sentence but is not the main idea.

C is incorrect. This information is given in the text to support the main idea.

D is incorrect. This information is not in the text so cannot be the main idea.

8 To solve this question we must work backwards. If 13 people were left after half the students got on the second bus, there must have been 26 students waiting, as 13 is half of 26. The 6 students who got on the first bus must be added to this to find the number of students who were waiting before the first bus came. There were 26 + 6 = 32 students.

9 The information tells us that everyone who liked safari also liked Smurfs and no-one who liked Smurfs liked pandas. So it is reasonable to draw the conclusion that if Thao likes safari, he also likes Smurfs and so does not like pandas.

A is incorrect. The information tells us that everyone who liked safari also liked Smurfs.

B is incorrect. There is not enough information to draw this conclusion so we cannot say it must be true.

D is incorrect. The information tells us that everyone who liked Smurfs also liked hot dogs, but it does not follow that everyone who likes hot dogs also likes Smurfs.

10 First work out how many customers each serves in an hour.

Karl: 1 customer in 20 minutes
             $\times 3$ $\times 3$
             3 customers in 60 minutes

Milla: 1 customer in 15 minutes
             $\times 4$ $\times 4$
             4 customers in 60 minutes

Priya: 2 customers in 60 minutes

Then add these numbers to work out how many customers can be served in an hour by Karl, Milla and Priya. Together they can serve 3 + 4 + 2 = 9 customers per hour. Multiply this by 8 hours to get 72 customers.

Together: 9 customers in 1 hour
                 $\times 8$ $\times 8$
                 72 customers in 8 hours

11 For Summer's conclusion to hold, it must be assumed that anyone who carries a fishing rod must fish: Carlos is carrying a fishing rod to the river + anyone who carries a fishing rod must fish means therefore Carlos fishes.

A is incorrect. This is the evidence Summer has used to draw her conclusion.

B is incorrect. This is Summer's conclusion, not the missing assumption.

C is incorrect. This is the real reason why Carlos is carrying the fishing rod, not the assumption that Summer has made.

12 A is incorrect. Notice where the trees in the original image are placed. There is one right at the top of the left hill. This means there should be one at the top of the right hill when we look from the other side.

C is incorrect. The hill itself is the wrong shape.

D is incorrect. There should only be two trees on the left hillside but in this image there are three.

13 To start with there are 100 drinks served to 80 people. Five people have no drinks so there are really 100 drinks served to 75 people. If 11 people have 3 drinks each, there are 67 drinks $(100 - 3 \times 11 = 67)$ served to 64 $(75 - 11 = 64)$ people.

The remaining people are served either 1 or 2 drinks. To find out how many had 2 drinks we find the difference between 67 drinks and 64 people, which is 3. So 3 people are served 2 drinks and 61 people $(64 - 3 = 61)$ are served only one drink.

14 Tom assumes that since eight singing competitions were won by students at his school during the year, there were eight students who won those competitions. However, it may be that some students won more than one competition, which would mean fewer than half of the qualifiers could be competition winners. So C shows the flaw in Tom's reasoning.

A is incorrect. This statement might be true but it is not a mistake Tom has made.

B and D are incorrect. These statements could be true but they are irrelevant to Tom's claim and not mistakes he has made.

15 Ariane claims that bringing her dog to work would reduce stress and boost productivity in the workplace. However, if a colleague is allergic to dogs, their stress levels could be increased and productivity decreased. So this statement contradicts, and therefore weakens, Ariane's claim.

B is incorrect. This statement neither strengthens nor weakens the claim about stress levels and productivity on the workplace.

C is incorrect. This statement could strengthen Ariane's argument.

D is incorrect. This statement could potentially weaken Ariane's general argument in favour of a pet-friendly workplace but it does not **most** weaken her argument about reducing stress and boosting productivity in the workplace.

16 Option C, that maintenance of the garden will be virtually nil, undermines Mr Small's claim that the garden will become overgrown and dangerous because no-one will want to look after it. Therefore this statement most weakens his argument.

A is incorrect. This statement may be true but it does not weaken Mr Small's argument that the garden will become overgrown and dangerous because no-one will want to look after it.

B is incorrect. This is a restatement of a comment Mr Small has already made so it doesn't weaken the argument.

D is incorrect. This statement is irrelevant to Mr Small's claim that the garden will become overgrown and dangerous because no-one will want to look after it.

17 To find the answer we need to work backwards. In the third game he lost one-third of his cards and was left with 20. As 20 represents two-thirds, the one-third he lost must have been 10 cards. Xavier must have started the third game with 30 cards.

Before the second game he must have had 38 cards, as he lost 8 cards to be left with 30.

Before the first game he must have had 19 cards, as he doubled this to be left with 38.

18 We need to find out who scored lowest by reading only those parts of the statements that relate to marks.

From the first and third statements, it is clear Ahmed got a lower mark than Bethany and Chloe. From the last statement, we can see

Dustin got a lower mark than Ahmed. So Dustin got the lowest mark.

Now we need to find out how fast Dustin finished the test.

From the fourth statement, we see that Dustin finished the test faster than Ahmed. From the first statement, we see that Ahmed was faster than Bethany. From the third statement, we see that Bethany was faster than Chloe. This means Dustin was faster than everyone else. He finished the fastest.

19 This outcome is not possible. If Shayna passed scales, then she must have passed at least one other extra component. Shayna cannot have passed sight reading because everyone who passed sight reading also passed the aural test. If this were true, it would mean that Shayna had passed all three components—but the information tells us that no-one passed all three components.

B is incorrect. This outcome could be true. Shayna could have failed scales and sight reading but still passed the aural test.

C is incorrect. This outcome could be true. Just because no-one who passed sight reading failed the aural test, it does not mean that someone didn't pass the aural test but failed sight reading.

D is incorrect. This outcome could be true. If Shayna passed scales, then she must have passed at least one other extra component. Shayna cannot have passed sight reading because everyone who passed sight reading also passed the aural test. If this were true, it would mean that Shayna had passed all three components. However, the information tells us that no-one passed all three components. So Shayna could have passed scales and the aural test.

20 Both Ria's and David's reasoning is correct.

Ria is correct because if the scores for presentation were different but the scores for taste were the same, then their final scores could not be equal.

David is correct because if the scores for presentation were the same but the scores for taste were different, then their final scores could not be equal.

The other options are incorrect by a process of elimination.

SAMPLE TEST 4A

Page 59

1 A 2 A 3 C 4 D 5 B 6 D 7 A 8 B 9 C
10 B 11 D 12 B 13 A 14 D 15 B 16 D
17 B 18 C 19 D 20 C

1 Ivan is going to the show for 6 days over a period of 8 days. There are many ways he can buy passes.

Buying a 5-day pass ($50) and two 1-day passes ($34) will cost $84 and will cover all of Ivan's dates. Buying a 5-day pass ($50) and a 3-day pass ($35) will cost $85. Buying two 3-day passes ($70) and a 1-day pass ($17) will cost $87. Buying a 3-day pass ($35) and three 1-day passes ($51) will cost $86.

2 Tim's conclusion is that it is Mimi's birthday today. He has based this conclusion on the evidence that Mimi is carrying a cake to school. So for his conclusion to hold, it must be assumed that students only bring cake to school on their birthday: Mimi is carrying a cake to school + students only bring cake to school on their birthday means therefore it is Mimi's birthday.

B is incorrect. This is Tim's conclusion.

C is incorrect. This would not support a conclusion that it is Mimi's birthday today.

D is incorrect. This is the evidence Tim used to draw his conclusion.

3 Sophie has completed all eight quizzes. However, she says she will win a prize for sure whereas Mr Lee says that completing the eight quizzes gives only a **chance** of winning a prize. So this option shows the mistake Sophie has made.

A is incorrect. This statement is irrelevant to winning a prize and is not a mistake Sophie has made.

B is incorrect. Mr Lee does not say anything about where the quizzes had to be completed and this is not a mistake Sophie has made.

D is incorrect. This statement is not a mistake made by Sophie.

4 After a rotation to the right, you can see that D is the answer.

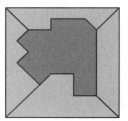

5 Since Zoe had a record of previous school service, the result of the Science test was not relevant in her case. She only had to pass the community-service challenge in order to attend the sustainability workshop. Since she was not selected to attend, she must have failed the community-service challenge.

A is incorrect. This statement might be true. However, since Zoe had a record of previous school service the result of the Science test was not relevant in her case. So it cannot be the reason she was not selected.

C is incorrect. The question tells us that Zoe had a good record of previous school service.

D is incorrect. Since Zoe had a record of previous school service, she only had to pass the community-service challenge to be selected to attend the workshop. So this statement that she did well in the challenge cannot be true since Zoe failed to be selected. Since it cannot be true, it cannot be the reason.

6 **A is incorrect.** A and D are very similar, except that in A the square and circle in the middle of the door have been swapped. Therefore the answer is D.

B is incorrect. It is just a rotation of the outside view.

C is incorrect. The big circle and a triangle are in opposite corners.

7 Light brown and dark brown make up exactly half so must be either sectors 6 and 1 or sectors 6 and 5.

The same number of people have blond hair as dark brown so dark brown cannot be sector 6 as it is the only sector of that size. So dark brown and blond are sectors 1 and 5. Sector 6 is light brown.

Red hair and other make up **less than** a quarter so they must be either sectors 2 and 3 or sectors 2 and 4 (sectors 3 and 4 are the same size). No other combination makes up **less than** a quarter.

Those with blond hair and red hair make up exactly a quarter. We know that blond must be sectors 1 or 5. We can see that sector 1 (or sector 5) and sector 2 make up exactly a quarter so sector 2 must be red.

This means sectors 3 and 4 represent black and other.

8 The club has at least two of each type of boat. Two quads, two doubles and two singles would be 6 boats and 14 rowers. There are 2 more boats and 3 more rowers. So there must be one more double and one more single.

9 Option C provides examples of how social media causes harm so it most strengthens Adam's argument that technology has some negative impacts on society.

A is incorrect. This statement neither strengthens nor weakens Adam's argument that technology has some negative impacts on society.

B is incorrect. Adam has already mentioned that technology can have negative impacts if it is misused. So this statement does not **most** strengthen his argument.

D is incorrect. This supports Adam's statement that these negative impacts exist but it does not **most** strengthen his argument.

10 This outcome is not possible. We are told that if there are not enough volunteers, then the fair will not be a success and if it isn't a success, then they will not be allowed to hold another fair. So if they did not have enough volunteers, then the fair cannot have been a success and so the principal would not have let them have a fair next term.

A is incorrect. It is possible that they had enough volunteers but that the fair was not successful for some other reason.

C is incorrect. It is possible that the fair was cancelled for some other reason.

D is incorrect. There is nothing in the information to tell us that this outcome is not possible.

11 Neither Matt's nor Kiah's reasoning is correct.

Matt says that Beau will be a successful puppy educator **for sure** and Matt does appear to have the qualities needed. However, the information does not say that someone with those qualities will **definitely** be a successful assistance dog puppy trainer. Matt's reasoning is therefore flawed.

Kiah's reasoning is also flawed. Kiah tells us that Madi loves a challenge, makes friends and helps others but that she doesn't think Madi likes dogs. Since Kiah does not know for sure that Madi does not like dogs, she cannot say that being a puppy educator is **definitely** not for Madi.

The other options are incorrect by a process of elimination.

12 Freetown is behind both other cities so it is on the far left. Tokyo is furthest ahead so it goes on the far right. The mini map should look like this:

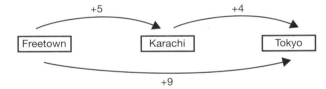

Tokyo is 4 hours ahead of Karachi. So we take 4 hours from 11:00 pm in Tokyo to get 7:00 pm in Karachi on the same day.

13 The main idea that the creator of the text wants us to accept is that ugly species, not just cute species, need our love and help to survive. The rest of the text gives more information to support this main idea.

B is incorrect. This background information is mentioned in the text but it is not the main idea.

C is incorrect. This information is not in the text so it cannot be the main idea.

D is incorrect. The information is given in the text to support the main idea.

14 The garden centre owner claims that even though the redevelopment will have increased capacity, it will improve the streetscape and enhance the surrounding locality. However, the statement that the area is already under stress with too much traffic contradicts, and therefore weakens, this claim.

A is incorrect. This statement could strengthen the garden centre owner's argument.

B is incorrect. This statement neither strengthens nor weakens the claim about improving the streetscape and enhancing the surrounding locality.

C is incorrect. This statement could potentially weaken an argument in favour of including a pet store in the redevelopment but it does not **most** weaken the argument about improving the streetscape and enhancing the surrounding locality.

15 We need to find out who the shortest person is by focusing only on the parts of each statement that mention age.

From the first two statements we can see that Emma is younger than Fiona and Greg is younger than Emma. This means Greg is younger than both Emma and Fiona. From the third statement we see that Harry is older than Fiona. This means Greg is younger than everyone.

Now we need to find out where Greg is in terms of height.

From the first statement we can see that Emma is taller than Greg. So he cannot be the tallest. Greg is taller than Harry so he cannot be the shortest. From the last statement we see that Fiona is shorter than Harry, who is shorter than Greg. Greg must be the second tallest.

16 Neither Garry's nor Kai's reasoning is correct. Garry says that they need to convince Lisa to return in order to qualify. However, the information does not say that teams qualifying because they came first or second in a regional competition must have the same team members. It only tells us that if the team is qualifying because it won the State Debating Challenge last year, then it needs to have the same members in the team this year. So Garry's reasoning is not correct and their team would qualify automatically. Kai's reasoning is also not correct. Since their team would qualify

automatically, it would not be eligible for the wild card draw and could not qualify by that means as he says it could.

A, B and C are incorrect by a process of elimination.

17 If Sonny makes 36 out of 60 burgers in 90 minutes, then Shubham must have made the other 24 burgers, as $60 - 36 = 24$. So Shubham makes 24 burgers in 90 minutes. This means he makes 8 burgers every 30 minutes and 16 burgers every hour.

Shubham: 24 burgers in 90 minutes
           ÷ 3   ÷ 3
        8 burgers in 30 minutes
           × 2   × 2
     16 burgers in 60 minutes

18 Seattle is the furthest behind so it goes on the left. Port Moresby is the furthest ahead so it goes on the right. The mini map should look like this:

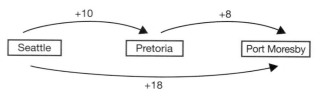

Port Moresby is 18 hours ahead of Seattle so we add 18 hours onto midday to get 6:00 am the next day. (12 hours ahead of midday is midnight. 6 hours ahead of midnight is 6 am.)

19 Mr Ceric did not assess students before the investigation started to establish which students were better spellers so he cannot state for a fact that walking improved the results. There could be any number of reasons for the results.

A is incorrect. It may be true that the L to Z group might have wanted to walk but this is not the teacher's mistake when he drew his conclusion.

B is incorrect. It may be true but it would not affect the results of the investigation because the teacher used the average result to draw his conclusion.

C is incorrect. This may be true but this is not the mistake made by Mr Ceric when he drew his conclusion.

20 Lyle can fill 5 wheelbarrows in 30 minutes. Kell can fill 2 wheelbarrows in 20 minutes or 1 wheelbarrow in 10 minutes or 3 wheelbarrows in 30 minutes. Together Lyle and Kell can fill 5 + 3 = 8 wheelbarrows in 30 minutes. It would take them half this time (15 minutes) to fill 4 wheelbarrows.

Lyle: 5 wheelbarrows in 30 minutes
         $\times 2$ $\times 2$
         10 wheelbarrows in 60 minutes

Kell: 2 wheelbarrows in 20 minutes
         $\times 3$ $\times 3$
         6 wheelbarrows in 60 minutes

Together: 16 wheelbarrows in 60 minutes
         $\div 4$ $\div 4$
         4 wheelbarrows in 15 minutes

SAMPLE TEST 4B
Page 64

1 D **2** B **3** B **4** B **5** A **6** A **7** A **8** C **9** A
10 C **11** D **12** C **13** D **14** C **15** D **16** C
17 B **18** A **19** D **20** A

1 The cheapest combination is to buy Deal 3 ($40) and two lots of Deal 1 (2 × $20). Together this is $80. His change is 90 – 80 = $10.

2 Kale's mother claims the ocean pool needs renovating. This statement shows a benefit of a renovated seawall at the pool and so gives further evidence to support her claim.

A is incorrect. This statement weakens rather than supports Kale's mother's claim.

C is incorrect. This statement could be the reason Kale's mother wrote the letter but it is not relevant to the claim that the pool needs renovating.

D is incorrect. This statement is not relevant to the claim that the pool needs renovating.

3 In each row, each arrow points in the opposite direction to the arrow to its left and right.

A is incorrect. The middle arrow should be pointing to the top right.

C is incorrect. The two arrows in the top of the nine missing tiles should point to the bottom right and then the top left.

D is incorrect. The bottom two arrows should be pointing to the top right and bottom left.

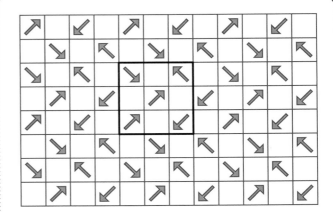

4 The main idea is that Surf Cove local council wants residents to report any fox sightings and B is the option that best expresses this. The rest of the text gives supporting information about why and how residents should report fox sightings.

A and D are incorrect. This is supporting information for the main idea.

C is incorrect. This information is not in the text so cannot be the main idea.

5 We need to work out which section of the graph represents which type of lolly.

The spotted section is three times the size of the dark-purple section (it is the only section three times the size of another). So the spotted section represents caramels and the dark-purple section represents chocolates.

There are three more lemon lollies than toffees so the white section is the lemon lollies and the light purple is the toffees. The one extra rectangle of the white section represents these 3 lollies. So each rectangle shows 3 lollies.

We need to find out which colour represents 12 lollies. If each rectangle represents 3 lollies, and 12 ÷ 3 = 4, then the colour showing 4 rectangles, the lemon, must represent 12 lollies.

There were 12 lemon lollies.

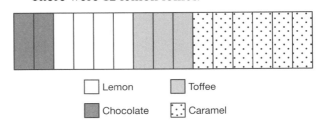

☐ Lemon   ☐ Toffee
■ Chocolate   ⋮ Caramel

6 If there are 12 guests left after $\frac{1}{3}$ of the guests leave, then 12 guests must represent $\frac{2}{3}$ of the guests that were in the restaurant.

If $\frac{2}{3}$ of the guests is 12, then $\frac{1}{3}$ of the guests is 6. This means there were 18 guests before $\frac{1}{3}$ of them left.

The 14 people who arrived need to be taken from this to find the number that were originally there: 18 − 14 = 4.

So there were four guests at the restaurant to begin with.

7 Zac's reasoning is correct when he says that something they spot and think **might** be a platypus **could** instead be a rakali.

B is incorrect. Stella's reasoning has a flaw. She reasons that if they can't see the tail, they won't be able to say for sure if it is a platypus or rakali. She has not thought that they might be close enough, the light might be good or they might get a look for long enough to identify a platypus without seeing its tail.

C and D are incorrect by a process of elimination.

8 Look at the difference between the times given. Hanoi is a full 13 hours ahead of Mexico City. Hanoi is 7 hours ahead of Edinburgh. Hanoi goes on the far right as it is ahead of both other cities. Mexico City is behind the other cities so goes on the left. The mini map might look like this:

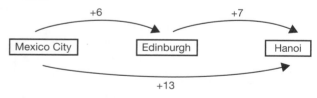

By subtracting 7 from 13 we can see that Edinburgh is 6 hours ahead of Mexico City.

9 If whoever grew the tallest plant must have had a garden position with both good sunlight and good soil, then it follows that anyone who does not satisfy both requirements cannot have grown the tallest plant. So if Emma did not have a position with good soil, she cannot have grown the tallest plant.

B is incorrect. Just because Nina satisfies both requirements, it does not mean she **must** have grown the tallest plant. There might also be others who satisfy both requirements. It only means that Nina **might** have grown the tallest plant.

C is incorrect. Just because James did not have a position with good sunlight, it does not mean he did not have a position with good soil.

D is incorrect. Just because Yusef did not grow the tallest plant, it does not mean he must not have had a position with good soil.

10 If Indira shears a sheep every 2 minutes, then in 1 hour she can shear 30 sheep, as 60 ÷ 2 = 30 sheep. This means Vashty must have shorn the other 20 sheep, as 50 − 30 = 20 sheep. If Vashty shears 20 sheep in 60 minutes (1 hour), then it takes her 3 minutes to shear a sheep, as 60 ÷ 20 = 3 minutes.

11 We know that any volunteers who did not work in the canteen last month **will** be put on the roster next month. However, that does not mean that anyone who worked in the canteen last month will definitely **not** be rostered to work again next month. So this sentence shows the flaw in Anita's father's reasoning and he may be rostered to work in the canteen again next month.

A is incorrect. This sentence is true and is not a mistake made by Anita's father.

B is incorrect. This sentence is a mistake since the supervisor said they definitely will be put on the roster next month. However, it is not a mistake made by Anita's father.

C is incorrect. This sentence is true and is not a mistake made by Anita's father.

12 **A is incorrect.** The shape in the middle of the top of the door is not flipped.

B is incorrect. The middle row of shapes is not changed.

D is incorrect. The triangle in the top corner is facing the wrong way.

13 Draw a simple Venn diagram. The rectangle holds all 9 teams. Two overlapping circles will hold the teams with red and the teams with white.

The one team that has no red or white goes outside the circles but inside the rectangle. This leaves 9 – 1 = 8 teams to go inside the circles.

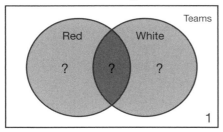

We are told that 5 have red and 6 have white. This is 5 + 6 = 11 teams to fill 8 spots inside the circles. So 3 teams are counted twice, as 11 – 8 = 3. Three teams go inside the overlapping part of the circle.

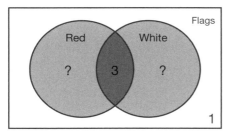

So, of the 6 teams that have white, 3 teams have red as well, leaving 3 teams that have white but not red.

The complete Venn diagram is shown below.

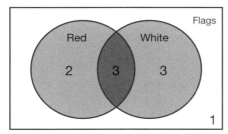

14 This statement cannot be true. Gemma was second to guess the word but was slower than Lee so Lee must have been first to guess the word.

A is incorrect. This statement could be true. So it is not possible to state it **cannot** be true.

B is incorrect. This statement is true.

D is incorrect. We don't know whether this statement is true or not, since we do not know how many rows Molly used. So it is not possible to state it **cannot** be true.

Making a table will help.

Name	Fastest time to guess the word	Rows needed to guess the word
Lee	1st	6
Gemma	2nd	5
Gary	3rd or 4th	3 or 4
Molly	3rd or 4th	Not known
Baye	5th	3

15 The writer of the argument in the box wants you to accept that guinea pigs have needs and are not just an easy, no-care pet. The writer begins the text with this claim, then provides evidence or reasons to support the claim and ends with a call to action. Text D uses this same structure. It begins with a claim (adopt a pet instead of buying one), then provides evidence to support the claim (it will save a life) and ends with a call to action (visit today).

A and B are incorrect. These texts state a claim and give reasons to support the claim. However, they do not conclude with a call to action.

C is incorrect. This text states a claim and gives reasons to support this claim. However, it concludes with a restatement of the claim rather than a call to action.

16 We need to find out who knocked over the most hurdles.

From the first statement, Kim knocked over fewer hurdles than Monica, so it can't be Kim. The second statement tells us that it can't be Neville as Lawrence knocked over more hurdles than him. This means it must be Monica or Lawrence but the third statement tells us than Monica knocked over more hurdles than Lawrence. Monica knocked over the most hurdles.

Now we must find out where Monica finished.

From the first and fourth statements, we can see that Neville finished ahead of Kim, who finished ahead of Monica. Monica came 3rd or 4th. From the third statement we see that Monica finished ahead of Lawrence. She came 3rd in the race.

17 You can work out that a Council gardener does not attend when the sprinklers are used so it could be Tuesday, Thursday, Friday or Sunday. The only option that must be true is that the day is Friday and the gardener is not onsite because the automatic sprinklers water on Fridays from 3 am to 4:30 am.

A is incorrect. The information states that the gardener waters from 7:30 am until 8:30 am so, if the gardener was not onsite watering, it cannot have been a day the garden was meant to be watered by the gardener.

C is incorrect. There is no information to support this conclusion. The question asks which option must be correct and not which one might be correct.

D is incorrect. Watering occurs every day, either automatically or by hand.

18 We need to find the farmer with the fewest cattle.

From the first and fourth statements we can see that Heather has fewer cattle than Francis and Ingrid. From the second statement we see that Grant has more cattle than Ingrid. So Heather has the fewest cattle.

Now we need to find out how many sheep Heather has compared to the others.

From the first and second statements we see that Heather has more sheep than Francis and Grant. The fourth statement tells us that Francis has more sheep than Ingrid so Heather must have more sheep than all of them. She has the most sheep.

19 Both Dani and Evie use incorrect reasoning. Dani uses incorrect reasoning because she cannot definitely conclude that Carly took the Coolibah Route based on it being a long trek. Carly might have taken the Waratah Route, which was longer. You should judge that each route is a long trek to the lookout. Evie uses incorrect reasoning because the rope bridge is on the Keating's Ridge Route. Carly might have taken the Coolibah Route. Other answers are incorrect by a process of elimination.

20 The camera at Horton St Hobby Shop can stay longer underwater than any of the other cameras. It is also the lightest of the cameras.

B is incorrect. The camera at City Cameras is the heaviest so Robert will not buy it.

C is incorrect. The camera at Bill's Cameras spends 30 minutes less underwater than the camera at Horton St Hobby Shop.

D is incorrect. The Smith's Electrical camera would be Robert's second choice. It is slightly heavier and stays underwater five minutes less than the camera at Horton St Hobby Shop.